e-tron
W0372460
S 700 NZ

Inhalt

Salzburg Stadt & Land
Ausgabe No. 2

FOKUS & FAKTEN
Focus & Facts

SHOPPING & LIFESTYLE
Shopping & Lifestyle

HOME & DESIGN

Home & Design

KUNST & KULTUR

Art & Culture

KULINARIK & GENUSS

Cuisine & Delights

GUIDE

Guide

Guide-Rubriken / *Guide Categories*

Shopping & Lifestyle Guide

Restaurant & Hotel Guide

Magazin-Rubriken / *Magazine Categories*

Fokus & Fakten
Focus & Facts

Shopping & Lifestyle
Shopping & Lifestyle

Home & Design
Home & Design

Kulinarik & Genuss
Cuisine & Delights

Kunst & Kultur
Art & Culture

Guide

Legende

Story

Interview

FOLLOW LA LOUPE

@laloupe

@laloupemagazine

laloupe.shop

SICH ZEIT NEHMEN ...

Taking your time ...

dt. / Mönch Haemin Sunim sagte einmal: „Die schönen Dinge siehst du nur, wenn du langsam gehst." Besonders bei nächtlichen Spaziergängen, wenn sich der Trubel gelegt hat und das Licht der Schaufenster auf das Kopfsteinpflaster der Altstadt fällt, genießen wir die andere Sicht auf die Dinge. Nicht ohne Zufall finden sich so neue Lieblingsstücke in den Schaufenstern, auch manch Begegnungen finden ihren Platz in unseren Gedanken, um ihre wahre Schönheit zu zeigen. Gute Dinge die Zeiten überdauern lassen oder Alltagsgegenständen eine neue Identität geben – schlussendlich stehen dahinter immer Menschen, die weiterdenken. Die dafür Sorge tragen, dass eine Lederhose nicht aus der Mode kommt oder eine Wasserflasche mehr als nur ein Alltagsgegenstand bleibt. Die Tag für Tag unter Beweis stellen, dass Tradition zeitgemäß ist. Und bestimmt noch lange Freude machen, Leidenschaft entfachen und Stoff für gute Geschichten liefern wird.

Wir schenken Ihnen gerne ein bisschen Zeit in Salzburg Stadt & Land!

engl. / It was Monk Haemin Sunim who once said: "Beauty will only reveal itself when we walk slowly." And that is especially true for night-time walks, when the hustle and bustle and has died down and the lights of the shop windows illuminate the old town's cobblestones – that's when we enjoy a completely different perspective of things. It's no coincidence that that's how we come across new favourite pieces in shop windows or how some encounters find their way into our thoughts to reveal their true beauty. Good things that last or everyday items that get a new identity – in the end it's always people who think ahead that stand behind them. Who make sure that a pair of lederhosen doesn't go out of fashion or a water bottle is more than just an everyday object. Who prove, every single day, that tradition is fashionable. And who kindle passions and create good stories.

We're happy to present you with a little bit of time in Salzburg City & Province!

Julia & Benjamin Skardarasy
Herausgeber / *Editors*

bs@laloupe.com
+43 664 / 5413 907
www.laloupe.com

Instagram:
@laloupemagazine

SWISS DESIGN / HANDMADE IN JAPAN

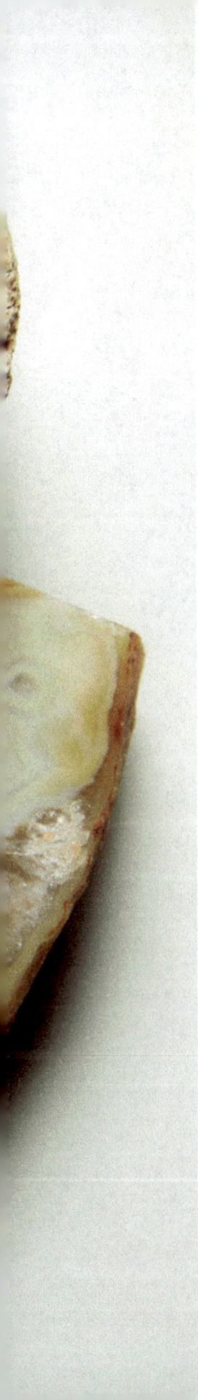

Fokus & Fakten

Focus & Facts

dt. / Sommer in Salzburg – das bedeutet Lebensfreude pur, ob auf einer blühenden Almwiese oder in einem der schönen Salzburger Cafés. Wir zeigen Ihnen außerdem genussvolle Plätze an den Salzburger Seen und verraten Ihnen fünf Erlebnisse im Salzburger Land, die Ihre Zeit hier noch schöner machen. Und unvergesslich. Willkommen in Salzburg!

engl. / Summer in Salzburg – stands for pure joie de vivre; be it on blooming alpine meadows or in one of Salzburg's beautiful cafés. We'll show you stunning spots by Salzburg's lakes and tell you about five experiences in the Salzburg region that'll make your time here even better. And truly unforgettable. Welcome to Salzburg!

GENUSS OHNE WORTE

Enjoyment without words

EVENTHIGHLIGHTS

Event highlights

8. Juni 2019

Sigmund-Haffner-Gassenfest

Es wird gemunkelt, die Sigmund-Haffner-Gasse mit ihrem italienischen Flair sei eine der schönsten Einkaufsstraßen der Stadt Salzburg. Beim Fashion-Event im Rahmen des bunten Gassenfestes Anfang Juni kann man sich davon selbst überzeugen – und bei den exklusiven Modeschauen die Kollektionen für die neue Saison entdecken.

---

7. – 10. Juni 2019

Salzburger Pfingstfestspiele

Im Juni startet mit den Pfingstfestspielen alljährlich die Festspielsaison in der Stadt Salzburg. Dieses Jahr wird den Gästen unter dem Motto „Voci celesti – Himmlische Stimmen" wieder ein großartiges Programm geboten – von Georg Friedrich Händels Oper „Alcina" über verschiedene Konzerte bis hin zum Film „Farinelli Il Castrato".

---

17. – 29. Juni 2019

Sommerszene Salzburg

Die Sommerszene ist seit vielen Jahren ein Fixpunkt am Salzburger Kulturhimmel. Diesmal steht das International Performing Arts Festival unter dem Motto „Now or Never" und bietet 15 Produktionen aus aller Welt, die mit ihren aktuellen Tanz- und Theaterstücken für knapp zwei Wochen in Salzburg gastieren.

---

28. & 29. Juni 2019

Altstadtfest Linzergasse

Alle Jahre wieder begeistert das Linzergassenfest Gäste wie Einheimische gleichermaßen. Die beliebte Gasse links der Salzach wird für zwei Tage zum Gastronomie- und Partyhotspot, mit Livebands und einem bunten Programm für Jung und Junggebliebene.

---

5. – 7. Juli 2019

UCI Trials World Cup

Ein spektakuläres Sportevent am Residenzplatz, mitten in der Altstadt. Die Union Cycliste Internationale (UCI) präsentiert mit den Trials eine besonders spannende Radsportdisziplin. Hauptfaktoren sind die Stabilität und Kontrolle des Fahrrads in Extremsituationen, in denen die Geschwindigkeit ebenfalls eine wichtige Rolle spielt.

---

19. & 20. Juli 2019
Fest zur Festspieleröffnung

„Die ganze Stadt soll Bühne sein", wünschte sich Fesspiel-Mitbegründer Max Reinhardt. Beim traditionellen Fest zur Festspieleröffnung wird diese Vision für Gäste wie Einheimische wahr. Zwei Tage wird in der ganzen Altstadt musiziert und performt – und das bei freiem Eintritt. Highlight: der berühmte Fackeltanz.

---

20. Juli – 31. Aug 2019
Salzburger Festspiele

Auch dieses Jahr versprechen die Salzburger Festspiele wieder ein Feuerwerk an künstlerischen Darbietungen mit vielen Stars, etwa Russel Thomas in Mozarts „Idomeneo", Sonya Yoncheva in Cherubinis „Médée" oder Cecilia Bartoli in Händels „Alcina". Auch Schauspiel und Konzerte werden begeistern, genauso wie der ewige Publikumsliebling „Jedermann".

---

12. Sept 2019
Salzburger Businesslauf

Sie laufen wieder! Am 12. September stellen sich Salzburger Unternehmen der sportlichen Herausforderung und bezwingen eine Strecke über 5,9 Kilometer. Dieses Jahr gibt es erstmals eine separate Nordic-Walking-Wertung. Start und Ziel ist der Residenzplatz im Herzen der Altstadt.

---

20. – 24. Sept 2019
43. Salzburger Rupertikirtag

Der Sommer der Hochkultur ist vorbei – im Herbst halten Tradition und Brauchtum Einzug in die Salzburger Altstadt. Der Rupertikirtag gilt als berühmtestes Volksfest im Bundesland. Musik, Handwerkskunst, Tracht, Markttreiben, Schausteller und natürlich das große Festzelt – hier wird bis in die Nacht hinein gefeiert!

---

5. Okt 2019
Lange Nacht der Museen

Im Zuge der „ORF Lange Nacht der Museen" öffnen wieder zahlreiche Museen und Galerien ihre Pforten. Von 18 Uhr bis 1 Uhr früh haben Kulturinteressierte die Möglichkeit, Ausstellungen zu besuchen und sich durch die Altstadt treiben zu lassen, von Galerien über das Künstlerhaus bis zum Museum der Moderne am Mönchsberg.

---

16. – 20. Okt 2019
Jazz & The City

Es jazzt und swingt wieder in Salzburg! Auf über 30 Bühnen, die in der gesamten Altstadt verteilt sind, geben sich nationale und internationale Stars der Jazzszene die Ehre. Das Jazz, World & Electronic Music-Festival bietet eine herrliche Vielfalt aus Tradition und internationaler Atmosphäre bei freiem Eintritt!

25. – 27. Okt 2019
Salzburg Trailrunning Festival

Cityflair und Mountainair – beim Salzburger Trailrunning Festival kommen Einsteiger wie Profis auf ihre Kosten. Kurze Strecken für Trail-Einsteiger und knackige Herausforderungen für Experten – an diesen zwei Tagen wird alles geboten, was das Trail-Laufherz höherschlagen lässt.

8 June 2019
Sigmund-Haffner street festival

Word has it that its Italian flair makes Sigmund-Haffner street one of the city of Salzburg's most beautiful shopping streets. During the fashion event which is part of the colourful street festival at the beginning of June you can see for yourself – and discover the new season's collections at exclusive fashion shows.

7 – 10 June 2019
Salzburg's Pentecost festival

The annual festival season in the city of Salzburg starts in June, with the Pentecost festival. This year guests will be entertained under the motto "Voci celesti – Heavenly Voices" and the programme is amazing – from Georg Frederick Handel's opera "Alcina" to various concerts all the way to the film "Farinelli Il Castrato".

17 – 29 June 2019
Sommerszene Salzburg

Salzburg's performing arts festival "Sommerszene" has been a fixed point in Salzburg's cultural calendar for many years. This year it will be all about the motto „Now or Never"; presenting 15 productions from all over the world that perform their latest dance and theatre pieces in Salzburg for almost two weeks.

---

28 & 29 June 2019

Old town festival Linzergasse

Every year the Linzergasse festival amazes both guests and locals. The popular street to the left of Salzach river becomes a crowded culinary and party hotspot for two days – with live bands and a colourful programme for the young and the young at heart.

---

5 – 7 July 2019

UCI Trials World Cup

A spectacular sports event that takes place on Residenzplatz, right at the centre of the old town. Union Cycliste Internationale (UCI) presents the Trials, a particularly exciting cycling discipline. The main factors are stability and control of the bike under extreme conditions, while speed also plays an important role.

---

19 & 20 July 2019

Festival Opening Party

"The entire town shall be our stage" was a wish one of the Salzburg Festival's co-founders, Max Reinhard, uttered. During the traditional celebration for the Festival opening this vision becomes true for guests and locals alike. For two days the entire old town will see music and performances – free of charge. Highlight: the famous torch dance.

---

20 July – 31 Aug 2019

Salzburg Festival

This year the Salzburg Festival once again promises to be a true firework of artistic performances with a great number of stars like Russel Thomas in Mozart's "Idomeneo", Sonya Yoncheva in Cherubini's "Médée" or Cecilia Bartoli in Handel's "Alcina". Theatre productions and concerts are also bound to amaze guests, just like the eternal crowd-pleaser "Jedermann".

---

12 Sept 2019

Business Run Salzburg

They're running again! On 12 September Salzburg's businesses will once more take on the athletic challenge and cover a stretch of 5.9 kilometres. This year will see a separate Nordic Walking discipline for the first time. Start and finish are on Residenzplatz, at the heart of the old town.

---

20 – 24 Sept 2019

43rd Ruperti fair Salzburg

The summer of high culture is passed – in autumn tradition and custom will once more pervade Salzburg's old town. The Rupertikirtag fair is seen as the whole province's most famous folk festival. Music, craftsmanship, traditional costume, busy markets, buskers and the huge festival tent – perfect for dancing the night away!

5 Oct 2019

Long Night of Museums

As part of the "ORF Long Night of Museums" numerous museums and galleries will once again open their doors. From 6 pm to 1 am culture lovers get the chance to see exhibitions and drift through the old town, from galleries to Künstlerhaus all the way to the Museum of Modern Art on Mönchsberg.

16 – 20 Oct 2019

Jazz & The City

Once again Salzburg will be all about jazz and swing! On the more than 30 stages, spread out over the entire old town, national and international stars of the jazz scene will offer their best performances. The Jazz, World & Electronic Music Festival shows off a wonderful variety of tradition and international atmosphere – free of charge.

25 – 27 Oct 2019

Salzburg Trailrunning Festival

City flair and mountain air – at Salzburg's trail running festival newbies as well as pros will get exactly what they're looking for. Short routes for trail beginners and proper challenges for experts – these two days offer everything a "runners' heart" could desire.

5 UNVERGESSLICHE ERLEBNISSE ...

5 unforgettable experiences ...

... am Land.
... in the country.

1. Die Altstadt von Hallein entdecken

Lange Zeit war sie die kleine Schwester von Salzburg, heute erlebt die Salz- und Keltenstadt einen zweiten Frühling. Zu Recht! Mittelalterliche Gassen, moderne Galerien, individuelle Shops oder das berühmte Café Braun – beim Spaziergang durch die Halleiner Altstadt findet man viele Schätze!

2. Beim Waldbaden im Gasteinertal der Natur ganz nah sein

Tief einatmen. Den Duft nach Moos und Waldblumen wahrnehmen. Dem Wind lauschen, wie er leise in den Blättern raschelt. Und genussvoll ausatmen. Waldbaden in Bad Hofgastein ist Wellness für Körper und Seele. Hier kommt man der Natur ganz nah – und auch sich selbst.

3. Prickelnd erfrischt werden im Felsenbad

Das wildromantische Felsenbad ist ein ewiger Geheimtipp. Versteckt zwischen Faistenau und dem Strüblweiher-Stausee, schlängelt sich das Flussbad pittoresk durch die Wälder. Auf den von der Sonne erwärmten Steinplatten liegen, dem Sommerkonzert der Vögel lauschen – und genießen.

4. Sich mit Schokolade zum Frühstück den Tag versüßen

Zugegeben: Bridget Jones hatte bestimmt nicht so einen luxuriösen Schokoladen-Brunch, wie er in Lofer serviert wird. In „Bergers Feinheit" genießt man das herrliche Alpenpanorama, während Schokolade in allen möglichen Geschmacks- und Darreichungsformen an den Tisch gebracht wird – von süß bis herzhaft.

5. Beim Sundowner den Gipfel der Gefühle erklimmen

Wenn die Sonne gerade hinter den Bergspitzen verschwindet, der eigens kreierte Sprudel im Glas perlt und aus der Küche verführerische Düfte dringen, ist man am Gipfel der Gefühle angelangt – auf der TOM Almhütte hoch über Maria Alm. Hinauf geht´s mit der Natrunbahn.

---

1. Disover Hallein's old town

For the longest time it was seen as "only" Salzburg's little sister – today the city of salt and Celts is seeing its second spring. And rightfully so! Medieval alleyways, modern galleries, individual shops, or the famous Café Braun – a stroll through Hallein's old town reveals many treasures.

---

2. Get close to nature during a dip in the forest pools at Gasteinertal valley

Take a deep breath. Breathe out with gusto. Notice the smell of moss and forest flowers. Listen to the wind as it rustles quietly in the trees. Going for a swim at Waldbad Bad Hofgastein is like being in a forest spa for body, mind, and soul. The two designated bathing areas are perfect for getting close to nature – and yourself.

---

3. Enjoy sparkling refreshment at the Felsenbad pool

The wild and romantic Felsenbad pool is an insider tip. Tucked away between Faistenau and the Strüblweiher reservoir the river pool winds its way through the forests. Simply stretch out on a warm slab of rock, listen to the birds' summer concert – and enjoy.

---

4. Have chocolate for breakfast and sweeten your day

Honestly: Bridget Jones probably did not have the kind of luxurious chocolate brunch that's served in Lofer. At Berger's Feinheit you can take in the stunning view of the surrounding mountains while being served chocolate in many different shapes and taste varieties – from sweet to savoury.

---

5. Reach emotional peaks with a sundowner-

When the sun is just about to disappear behind the mountains, the special-made bubbly fizzes in your glass and lovely smells from the kitchen tickle your nose, then you've reached the peak of emotions – at TOM Almhütte, high up above Maria Alm. Natrunbahn cable car is a comfortable way of getting up there.

MARTINI
SPORTSWEAR AUSTRIA
DESIGN
YOUR
SPORTS.

MARTINI SHOP
A-5524 ANNABERG 133
TELEFON: +43 6463 8171-22
MARTINI-SPORTSWEAR.COM

WILLKOMMEN AM SEE

Welcome by the lake

Ob glasklarer Gebirgssee oder zauberhafter Moorsee, mit (kulinarischem) Entertainment oder Natur pur: Die Salzburger Seen sind so vielfältig wie die Blautöne in ihren Fluten. Eines ist ihnen aber allen gemein: Man kann im wahrsten Sinne des Wortes in Schönheit baden.

Das Salzburger Land ist berühmt für seine Seen. Schon Peter Alexander besang das „Weisse Rössl am Wolfgangsee" und Romy Schneider flanierte durch die Räume des historischen Schloss Fuschl. Aber auch abseits der berühmten Salzkammergut-Seen gibt es hier viel zu entdecken. Doch Vorsicht: Ein paar Stunden an den Salzburger Seen kann chronische Seensucht hervorrufen.

Wolfgangsee

Schon der erste Blick auf den Wolfgangsee raubt einem schier den Atem. Eingebettet zwischen Zwölferhorn und Schafberg ist er zweifellos einer der schönsten Seen im Salzburger Land. Herrlich: der Promenadenweg von St. Gilgen zum Gasthof Fürberg. Man spaziert direkt am Wasser entlang, kann an romantischen Buchten baden und anschließend beim Gasthof vorzüglich speisen.

Fuschlsee

Wie ein Edelstein schmiegt sich der Fuschlsee in die Landschaft des salzburgischen Salzkammergutes, sein Farbenspiel changiert von tropischem Türkis bis zu dunklem Blau. Tipp: beim Edenbergers Café ein Tretboot ausleihen und auf den See hinausschippern. Kommt man dann glücklich und entspannt wieder am Ufer kann, kann man direkt am See frischen Fisch oder saftigen Kuchen genießen, während die Wellen leise ans Ufer plätschern.

Mattsee

Der Mattsee ist Teil des Trumer Seenlandes, das nur knapp 20 Kilometer von der Stadt Salzburg entfernt liegt. Ein gelungener Tag am Mattsee beginnt mit einem Frühstück im Schlosscafé des Schloss Mattsee, das malerisch auf einer Halbinsel liegt. Danach ein paar Schritte am See entlangspazieren –bestimmt findet sich ein gemütliches Plätzchen zum Entspannen. →

Goldegger See

Optischer und kulinarischer Genuss gehen am Goldegger See einträchtig Hand in Hand. Nachdem man im wohltuenden Wasser des Moorsees seine Runden gezogen hat, kann man im Seehof von Sepp Schellhorn die ausgezeichnete Küche genießen. Das Restaurant HECHT! r120 wird derzeit mit zwei Hauben geführt.

Hintersee

Der saubere Naturbadesee ist ein Geheimtipp unter den Seen und bietet Natur pur. Direkten Zugang zum See hat man nur an drei öffentlichen Badeplätzen, wo sich der Trubel selbst im Hochsommer in Grenzen hält. Bis heute hält sich das Gerücht, das im Hintersee Ende des Zweiten Weltkriegs Nazi-Gold versenkt wurde. Spektakulär und mehr als ein Gerücht ist der Minigletscher unweit des Sees, die sogenannte Eiskappel im Grießbachgraben.

Wallersee

Der größte See des Salzburger Voralpenlandes ist relativ flach und erwärmt sich schnell. So ist der Wallersee eine gute Wahl für den Start in die Badesaison, etwa am Strandbad Neumarkt mit feinsandigen Naturbadestrand. Zur gepflegten Einkehr empfiehlt sich das Restaurant Weyringer, von dem aus man einen traumhaften Blick auf den See hat. Aus der Küche kommen ausgezeichnete Gerichte mit internationalen Einflüssen.

engl. / *Whether it's a crystal-clear mountain lake or an enchanted moor lake, boasting (culinary) entertainment or just pure nature: Salzburg's lakes are as varied as their waters' shades of blue. But, there is one thing they all have in common: you can simply bathe in their beauty.*

The Salzburger Land region is famous for its lakes. Even the renowned folk singer Peter Alexander sang about it in "The White Horse Inn" by wonderful Wolfgangsee lake, as Romy Schneider strolled through the historic rooms of Fuschl castle. And the region actually has much more to offer than the famous Salzkammergut lakes. Be warned: already a few hours by Salzburg's lakes can cause chronic yearning.

Wolfgangsee

The very first glimpse of Wolfgansee lake is truly breathtaking. Located in between Zwölferhorn and Schafberg, it is, without a doubt, one of the Salzburger Land's most beautiful lakes. Wonderful: the promenade way from St. Gilgen to Gasthof Fürberg. Stroll along the water's edge, take a dip in romantic bays, and enjoy a wonderful meal at the Fürberg inn afterwards. →

Fuschlsee

Fuschlsee lake is nestled into the landscape of Salzkammergut region like a gem, it's colours shimmer and vary from tropical turquoise to dark blue. A tip: rent a pedal boat at Edenberger's Café and head out onto the lake. Once you get back to the lakeshore, all happy and relaxed, you can immediately enjoy fresh fish from the lake or scrumptious cakes while the waves lap softly at the shore.

Mattsee

This lake is part of the Trumer lake scenery which is only about 20 kilometres from the city of Salzburg. A perfect day at Mattsee lake starts with breakfast at the Mattsee castle's Schlosscafé which is located on a picturesque peninsula. Afterwards, during a stroll along the lakeshore, you'll quickly find a cosy spot to relax.

Goldegger See

At lake Goldegger See visual and culinary pleasures go hand in hand. After having enjoyed the soothing waters of the moor lake, Sepp Schellhorn's Seehof is the perfect spot to enjoy culinary delights. The two-star restaurant HECHT! r120 truly deserves its accolades.

Hintersee

This beautifully clean natural bathing lake is an insider tip among the lakes and it offers a pure natural experience. There are only three public bathing spots that offer direct access to the lake and even during midsummer it's not terribly busy. Up until today rumours about Nazi-gold being hidden in the lake since the end of world war II stubbornly persist. Spectacular and definitely more than just a rumour: the miniature glacier near the lake, the so-called Eiskappel in Griessbachgraben valley.

Wallersee

The largest lake of Salzburg's alpine upland is relatively shallow and thus warms up quickly. Which makes Wallersee lake the perfect spot to start the bathing season, at Neumarkt Strandbad, for example, with its natural sandy beach. Restaurant Weyringer is the perfect spot for an excellent meal with a stunning view of the lake. The kitchen delivers excellent cuisine that boasts international influences.

Shopping & Lifestyle

Shopping & Lifestyle

dt. / Moderne Schatzsucher sind in der Salzburger Altstadt genau richtig. Ob Lieblingsstücke Made in Salzburg oder echte Handwerkskunst – ein Blick in die Shops lohnt in jedem Fall. Über Kunst am Kopf spricht Christian Sturmayr im Interview und warum eine Lederhose in Salzburg nie aus der Mode kommen wird, verraten Stefan Wimmer und Georg Klampfer.

engl. / Salzburg's old town is the perfect place for modern treasure hunters. Whether it's about new favourite pieces made in Salzburg or real craftsmanship – checking out the shops is definitely worth it. In his interview Christian Sturmayr speaks about art on the head and Stefan Wimmer and Georg Klampfer tell us why lederhosen will never go out of fashion in Salzburg.

AREA® 25 Jahre
area.at
Schauräume
5020 Salzburg
Bayerhamerstr. 5
4020 Linz
Stifterstr. 31
Tisch: e15 Kazimir
Untergestell verzinkt, Platte Eiche weiß geölt
Stuhl: e15 Houdini
seidengrau und lapisblau lackiert

SHERPA FILZTASCHE
erhältlich bei / *available at*
www.stillsegler.com

LOBSTERS TONIC WATER
erhältlich bei / *available at*
www.lobsters.at

La Loupe®

LIEBLINGS-STÜCKE

Favourites

TREVIANO SPIRITUOSENFLASCHE
erhältlich bei / *available at*
www.stillsegler.com

Foto: ©ebihara photography

HOOBERT NATUR-KOLA
klassik, koffeinfrei, tonicbitter, Rosé
Hoobert Kola-Manufaktur,
Universitätsplatz 11

hand kopf werk

MADE IN SALZBURG

Hand.Kopf.Werk. jeden Freitag bis 15. November

Die Geschichten zu vielen handgemachten Produkten erfahren Sie bis 15. November jeden Freitag im Rahmen der Veranstaltungsreihe HAND.KOPF.WERK.: mit Handwerkstouren, Workshops, Vorträgen usw. nur in der Salzburger Altstadt.

WANDHAKEN „HIRSCHKOPF“
handgeschmiedet,
Schlosserei Wieber,
Getreidegasse 28

Weitere Informationen: www.salzburg-altstadt.at/de/hand-kopf-werk

For more information, see: www.salzburg-altstadt.at

Fotos: ©Andreas Kolarik

TEPPICH UND TEPPICHPATSCHEN
Handweberei Rupert Weiss,
Getreidegasse 18a

Shopping & Lifestyle

MESSER AUS EINEM STÜCK

handgefertigt mit Griff aus Buchenholz
und mit Lederscheide,
Messermacher Kappeller,
Getreidegasse 21

HIRSCHLEDERHOSE MIT STICKEREI

Salzburger Heimatwerk,
Residenzplatz 9

REGENSCHIRM

Schirmmanufaktur Kirchtag,
Getreidegasse 22

HANDGEDRUCKTE PAPETERIE

Letterpress Manufaktur Salzburg
erhältlich bei s'Fachl,
Kaigasse 13

Fotos: ©Kirchtag, ©Bernhard Müller, ©Salzburger Heimatwerk, ©Messermacher Kappeller GmbH

HOCHZEITSBECHER

Handwerkskunst in Glas,
Sigmund-Haffner-Gasse 14

CITY-SHOPPER AUS RINDSLEDER

Taschnerwerkstatt Hladik,
Schanzlgasse 6

TAUFTALER

Goldschmied Alexander Pappernigg,
Sigmund-Haffner-Gasse 13

Fotos: ©Andreas Kolarik

HERRENGÜRTEL

Gürtelmacher Schliesselberger,
Dreifaltigkeitsgasse 4

OHRCLIPS MIT CITRIN
Galerie Baischer,
Linzer Gasse 40

FRUCHTZUCKERL
Zuckerlwerkstatt,
Wiener-Philharmoniker-Gasse 3

WERMUT
Likör- und Punschmanufaktur Sporer,
Getreidegasse 39

entgeltliche Einschaltung / Paid content

Fotos: ©Sporer, ©Zuckerlwerkstatt, ©Galerie Baischer

OPEN-AIR-SHOPPING-ERLEBNIS SALZBURGER ALTSTADT

Salzburg's old town: a shopping hotspot

dt. / Altehrwürdige Mauern und geschichtsträchtige Gassen, die grünen Salzachufer und nahen Stadtberge – diese gelungene Symbiose macht Salzburg zu einem der beliebtesten Ausflugsziele Österreichs. Besonders im Sommer blüht die Mozartstadt so richtig auf und versprüht dank der weltberühmten Festspiele internationales Flair. Egal ob linkes oder rechtes Altstadtufer – die engen Gassen nahe der Salzach verwandeln sich in den wärmeren Monaten zur stimmungsvollen Open-Air-Shoppingzone.

Nobles Design, zeitlose Eleganz und unverkennbarer Stil zeichnen sowohl die Salzburger Altstadt als auch ihr Fashion-Angebot aus. Über 350 moderne Shops, klassische Boutiquen, exklusive Trachtenausstatter und traditionsreiche Juweliere garantieren ein besonderes Shoppingerlebnis unter freiem Himmel. Mit Prada, Hermes, Longchamp, Tod's, Louis Vuitton, Boss, Aigner und vielen mehr ist in der Altstadt das „Who is Who" der internationalen Modebranche vertreten.

Shopping & Lifestyle

Weitere Informationen: www.salzburg-altstadt.at

engl. / The successful symbiosis between time-honoured walls, historic streets and alleys, the green banks of the Salzach river and the mountains close to the city is what makes Salzburg one of Austria's most popular destinations. In the summer months the city is at its most beautiful and it boasts an international atmosphere. The charming old town to both sides of the river Salzach, around Getreidegasse und Linzer Gasse, is the perfect place for open-air shopping.

TIPP: ALTSTADT-GUTSCHEINE

Das Geschenk mit über 600 Shopping- und Genussmöglichkeiten, jetzt online bestellen unter www.salzburg-altstadt.at. Erhältlich auch bei diversen Banken in der Altstadt, bei der Tourismusinfo am Mozartplatz und den Service Centern Verkehr.

These vouchers are the perfect gift – one that opens up more than 600 shopping and indulgence options. Order now on www.salzburg-altstadt.at. Also available at the old town's banks, at Tourismusinfo Mozartplatz and the Vekehr Service Centres.

Sophisticated design, timeless elegance, and uncompromising style – all this characterises both Salzburg's old town and its fashion offer. More than 350 modern shops, classic boutiques, exclusive traditional costume stores, and traditional jewellers guarantee a unique shopping experience out in the open. Labels like Prada, Hermes, Longchamp, Tod's, Louis Vuitton, Boss, Aigner prove that the old town really hosts the "who is who" of fashion.

For more information, see: www.salzburg-altstadt.at

MARTINI SPORTSWEAR

Design your sports.
The Summer is ready to start.

© Fotos: Martini Sportswear/Mirja Geh

dt. / Jeder Outdoorsportler ist auf der Suche nach seinem eigenen, individuellen Abenteuer. Um diese Momente wirklich besonders zu machen, arbeitet Martini Sportswear voller Leidenschaft mit den besten Materialien und schafft einen Produktmix, der allen Naturverliebten auf den Leib geschneidert ist.

Die Hightech-Funktionsmode vom Familienunternehmen aus Annaberg paart sportliche Einzigartigkeit mit Design und Performance. Mode made in Europe – für alle Outdoorenthusiasten, für alle, die ihren Sport lieben und ihn mit Martini zu einem speziellen Erlebnis machen wollen. Jedes Jahr zur gleichen Zeit kommt dieses drängende und doch so gute Gefühl: „Raus in die Welt!“ Auch die neue Sommerkollektion wurde mit unbändiger Passion

umgesetzt, mit dem Willen, eine überzeugende und einzigartige Kollektion herauszubringen. Begriffe wie Hike'n'Bike, Trail'n'Run, aber auch Wandern und Chill and Enjoy spiegeln die Kreation perfekt wider und das Ergebnis beeindruckt: Egal, wie man seine Aktivitäten erlebt, Martini bietet jedem Abenteurer sein für sich perfektes Equipment.
Summer, sun and good vibes.

Shopping & Lifestyle

engl. / Every outdoor sports fan is always on the hunt for their personal, individual adventure. And in order to make these moments even more exceptional Martini Sportswear pours all its passion into working with the best materials and creating a product mix that will literally fit nature lovers like a second skin.

The high-tech functional fashion made by the family-owned business from Annaberg pairs unique athletics with design and performance. Fashion made in Europe – for all outdoor enthusiasts, for those who love their sports and who want to make it a special experience with Martini. Every year at the same time we all get this urge, this overwhelming feeling of: "I need to go out into the world!" And the new summer collection was also realised with limitless passion and the will to produce a convincing and unique collection. Terms like hike'n'bike, trail'n'run but also hiking and "chill and enjoy" perfectly reflect the collection's characteristics and the result is impressive: no matter how you choose to experience your activity, Martini has the perfect equipment for every adventurer. Summer, sun and good vibes.

MARTINI SPORTSWEAR

Nr. 133, 5524 Annaberg
Tel. +43 6463 / 81710, Fax +43 6463 / 8171 77
info@martini-sportswear.at, www.martini-sportswear.com

SERVUS DIE WADLN

Alpine legwear – Alpine lifestyle

Ein Gespräch mit Stefan Wimmer von „Wimmer schneidert“ und Georg Klampfer, Initiator des LederhosenDonnerstag

A talk with Stefan Wimmer of “Wimmer schneidert” and Georg Klampfer, initiator of LederhosenDonnerstag

Shopping & Lifestyle

dt. / Lederhose und Dirndl gehören zu Salzburg wie Mozart und Festspiele. Dass Moderne und Tradition dabei einträchtig Hand in Hand gehen können, beweisen Stefan Wimmer und Georg Klampfer im La Loupe-Interview. Stefan Wimmer repräsentiert die neunte Generation der Trachtenmanufaktur „Wimmer schneidert" in Schleedorf. Einer, der insbesondere der Lederhose in der Stadt Salzburg zu einem neuen Hype verholfen hat, ist Georg Klampfer, Organisator des „LederhosenDonnerstag". Sein Ziel: die Tracht zurück in den Alltag zu bringen. Im La Loupe-Interview sprechen die beiden über ihren individuellen Zugang zur Tracht und verraten, wie viele Lederhosen sie im Schrank haben.

L.L. / **Herr Wimmer, „Wimmer schneidert" gibt es seit 1741, das Unternehmen wird bereits in der neunten Generation geführt. Was ist noch so wie damals und was ist heute anders als 1741?**

S.W. / Was bei uns über die Jahrhunderte gleichgeblieben ist, ist das regionale Denken. Wir versuchen nach wie vor, regionale Lieferanten für unsere Kollektionen zu gewinnen, kaufen Loden oder Leinen möglichst in der Region. Auch die Tatsache, dass wir ein familiengeführtes Einzelunternehmen sind, in dem man sich untereinander kennt, ist gleichgeblieben.

„Wenn man eine ordentliche Lederhose hat, die angepasst wurde, dann passt die immer, zu jedem Anlass und ein Leben lang."

Georg Klampfer

„Salzburg ist eine Trachtenstadt, davon profitieren wir seit Generationen."

Stefan Wimmer

L.L. / **Es gibt bei vielen Kollektionen Klassiker, die die Jahrhunderte überdauern. Gibt es bei der Tracht auch ein Masterpiece, das über die Jahrhunderte übernommen wurde?**

S.W. / Ja, das gibt es tatsächlich. Zum einen bei der Lederhose, da ist der Schnitt ja sehr klassisch – manchmal etwas kürzer, manchmal etwas länger. Aber das Hirschleder, das auf ursprüngliche Art und Weise gegerbt wurde oder auch die Stickmuster, das sind sehr traditionelle Dinge. →

„Heute wird handwerklich noch vieles so gemacht wir vor 100 oder 150 Jahren."

Stefan Wimmer

Da ist heute noch vieles so, wie es schon vor 100 oder 150 Jahren war. Auch ein Dirndl besteht immer aus einem Mieder, also dem engen Oberteil, und einem Rock, der einmal gezogen ist und einmal in Falten gelegt wurde. Es ändern sich die Farben oder die Ausschnitte, aber im Grunde ist es über die Jahrhunderte gleichgeblieben.

L.L. / **Georg, wann haben Sie Ihre erste Wimmer-Lederhose bekommen?**

G.K. / Als ich 19 Jahre alt war, wurde mir die erste Lederhose angeschneidert. Die habe ich damals zur Matura bekommen und die trage ich heute noch. Die erste Wimmer-Lederhose, die ich je gehabt hab, die habe ich von meinem Cousin geerbt. Ich glaube, da war ich sechs Jahre alt. Und vorher hat sie wahrscheinlich schon meinem Onkel gehört (lacht). Für mich war es von klein auf selbstverständlich, eine Lederhose zu besitzen. Mindestens eine.

WORDRAP MIT STEFAN WIMMER:

1741 oder 2019?
2019.

Mein Masterpiece?
Eine kurze, handgemachte Lederhose.

Das gebe ich an die zehnte Generation weiter:
Handwerkliches Wissen und Können.

Der grösste Irrglaube zur Lederhose?
Dass man sie nur zu Festtagen tragen kann.

L.L. / **Sie haben es geschafft, mit dem LederhosenDonnerstag in Salzburg die Tracht wieder modern zu machen. Wie haben Sie das gemacht, welche Idee stand dahinter?**

G.K. / Wenn ich ehrlich bin, hat es keine Idee dahinter gegeben (lacht). Ich habe einfach gerne die Lederhose angezogen. Mein Partner vom LederhosenDonnerstag, Christian Eibl, hat mal gesagt, dass er es toll findet, dass ich die Lederhose auch beruflich anziehe. Mit einem Sakko dazu passt das super ins Büro. Er wollte die Lederhose auch öfter im Alltag tragen, nicht immer nur zu Hochzeiten oder zum Rupertikirtag. So haben wir den LederhosenDonnerstag ins Leben gerufen. Ich denke damit geben wir den Leuten, die sich vielleicht nicht trauen, die Tracht auch unter der Woche anzuziehen, eine gute Möglichkeit, genau das zu tun. Und wenn dann jemand auf der Straße fragt: „Hey, warum hast du die Lederhose an?", dann kann man sagen: „Heute ist doch LederhosenDonnerstag". (lacht) Der Erfolg hat uns aber selbst überrascht.

„Für mich war es von klein auf selbstverständlich, eine Lederhose zu besitzen. Mindestens eine."

Georg Klampfer

Ich glaube, dass es auch deshalb so gut angekommen ist, weil es kein Marketinggag irgendeiner Firma war. Sondern weil einfach zwei Deppen jeden Donnerstag die Lederhose angezogen und Spaß gehabt haben (lacht).

L.L. / **Herr Wimmer, kann man eine Linie ziehen zwischen Alltagstracht und Festtagstracht?**

S.W. / Da hat sich in den letzten Jahren viel verändert. Die Tracht ist heute viel unkomplizierter als früher – da hat sicher der LederhosenDonnerstag einen Teil dazu beigetragen. Heute kann man eine Trachtenjacke zur Lederhose genauso anziehen wie zur Jeans.

G.K. / Da ist auch das Lässige: Man kann es in beide Richtungen kombinieren. Ob ich die festliche Jacke zur Jeans anziehe oder die Lederhose zum Polo – da passt beides. Das finde ich klasse. Auch beim LederhosenDonnerstag geht es ja nicht darum, dass jeder eine handgemachte Hirschlederne haben muss. Es geht darum, dass wir gemeinsam die Tracht feiern. Und wenn man eine Tracht anhat, ist es einfach gleich lustiger. →

„Wahrscheinlich hat es auch deshalb so gut funktioniert, weil der LederhosenDonnerstag kein Marketinggag war – sondern weil einfach zwei Deppen jeden Donnerstag die Lederhose angezogen haben."

Georg Klampfer

www.lederhosendonnerstag.at

Georg Klampfer ist Mitbegründer des LederhosenDonnerstag. Gemeinsam mit Christian Eibl setzt er sich dafür ein, dass die Lederhose wieder stärker das Strassenbild prägt. Seit 2015 laden die beiden Salzburger im Rahmen der Afterwork-Veranstaltungsreihe „Feierabendbier" regelmässig zu verschiedenen Locations in und rund um die Stadt Salzburg, um die Tracht zu feiern und den LederhosenDonnerstag bei einem gemütlichen Bier oder einem Glas Wein stilvoll ausklingen zu lassen. Unterstützt werden sie von ihren Vereinskollegen, die die Lederne genauso feiern wie die beiden.

Stefan Wimmer ist Geschäftsführer des traditionsreichen Familienbetriebs „Wimmer schneidert". Der Betrieb besteht seit 1741 – bis heute wird in der Schneiderei am ursprünglichen Standort in Schleedorf hochwertige Trachtenmode nach Mass gefertigt. In Salzburg kann man die Stücke im Rochushof erstehen. Individualität, Qualität und Regionalität sind wichtige Werte des Betriebs, der sich zum Ziel gesetzt hat, Tracht im 21. Jahrhundert nicht bloss „tragbar" zu gestalten, sondern vielmehr daraus Lieblingsstücke zu machen, die den Stil der Trägerin und des Trägers perfekt zum Ausdruck bringen.

„Tracht ist heute viel unkomplizierter als früher."

Stefan Wimmer

L.L. / **Und wie ist Tracht bei den Salzburger Festspielen etabliert?**

S.W. / Beim Jedermann gehen traditionell viele Gäste in Tracht, die Herren auch in der kurzen Lederhose. Bei Opernpremieren hat man eine lange Tracht an, ein festliches Dirndl oder eine lange Lederhose.

„Für den Mann ist die Lederhose, was für die Frau die Chanel-Tasche ist."

Georg Klampfer

L.L. / **Wie viele Lederhosen haben Sie?**

G.K. / Ich habe fünf, aber ich ziehe immer nur zwei, drei an. Das sind die, die handgemacht sind – die sitzen einfach anders. Wenn man eine ordentliche Lederhose hat, die angepasst wurde, dann passt die immer, zu jedem Anlass und ein Leben lang. Ich denke, die Lederhose ist für den Mann das, was für eine Frau eine Chanel-Handtasche ist.

S.W. / Ich habe drei kurze und eine lange Lederhose.

L.L. / **Wie lange muss man auf eine Wimmer-Lederhose im Regelfall warten?**

S.W. / Wenn man bei uns eine Lederhose machen lässt, dauert es bei handgemachten zwischen acht und neun Wochen. So lange kann man im Regelfall warten. Und ein bisschen Vorfreude ist ja auch schön.

STAMMHAUS SCHLEEDORF

Dorf 96, 5205 Schleedorf
Tel. +43 6216 / 6562

Öffnungszeiten:
Mo – Fr 8 – 12 Uhr und 13 – 18 Uhr
Sa 8 – 12 Uhr

GESCHÄFT SALZBURG

Rochusgasse 6, 5020 Salzburg
Tel. +43 662 / 8240 80

Öffnungszeiten:
Mo – Fr 9.30 – 18 Uhr
Sa 9 – 12.30 Uhr

lebensfreude@wimmertracht.at, www.wimmertracht.at

© Foto: Albrecht Schnabel

engl. / Lederhosen and Dirndl dresses are a part of Salzburg – just like Mozart and the Salzburg Festival. In their interview with La Loupe, Stefan Wimmer and Georg Klampfer prove that modern age and tradition can coexist quite peacefully here. Stefan Wimmer represents the ninth generation of the traditional costume manufacture "Wimmer schneidert" in Schleedorf. And Georg Klampfer has initiated a new hype around lederhosen in the city of Salzburg by organising the so-called "Leder-hosenDonnerstag" or LederhosenThursday. His goal: bringing traditional costume back into everyday life. In their interview with La Loupe the two talk about their individual approaches to traditional costume and let us know how many pairs of lederhosen they have in their closets. →

"Once you get a proper pair of lederhosen that was tailor-made for you it simply works – at every occasion and for the rest of your life."

Georg Klampfer

"The people of Salzburg have always been partial to traditional garb and we've been profiting from that for generations."

Stefan Wimmer

„Nowadays there still are many things that are made exactly the same way as 100 or 150 years ago."

Stefan Wimmer

L.L. / ***Mr. Wimmer, "Wimmer schneidert" was founded in 1741 and is now family-run in the ninth generation. What has remained the same and what has changed since 1741?***

S.W. / *One aspect that has remained unchanged across the centuries is the regional focus. We still try to find regional suppliers for our collections, and we try to buy loden and linen from the region. And the fact that we are a family-run individual business has not changed.*

© Foto: Albrecht Schnabel

L.L. / ***Many collections feature classics that never lose their popularity. Would you say that traditional costume also knows a certain masterpiece that has outlasted the centuries?***

S.W. / *Yes, I think so, actually. When it comes to lederhosen, the cut is a classic – sometimes they're a bit shorter, sometimes a bit longer. And the deerskin which was tanned using original processes as well as the stitching and patterns are all traditional elements. There are many things that have been the way they are today for 100 or 150 years. And a Dirndl dress is always made up of a bodice, so a tight top, and a skirt, which would sometimes be flowing and sometimes be pleated. The colours and necklines change, but basically it has remained the same for centuries.*

„For me it simply has always been natural to own lederhosen. At least one pair."

Georg Klampfer

www.lederhosendonnerstag.at

L.L. / ***Georg, when did you get your first pair of Wimmer Lederhosen?***

G.K. / *When I was 19 years old I got my first tailor-made pair of lederhosen. It was a gift after I'd finished my A-levels and I still wear it. The very first pair of Wimmer Lederhosen I had was a hand-me-down from my cousin though. I think I was six years old when I got it. And before me it probably belonged to my uncle (laughs). For me it was always natural that I had lederhosen. At least one pair.*

L.L. / ***By introducing LederhosenDonnerstag in Salzburg you managed to make the traditional costume hip again. How did you pull that off and what was the idea behind it?***

G.K. / *Honestly, there really wasn't much of an idea behind it (laughs). I simply enjoyed wearing my lederhosen. My LederhosenDonnerstag partner, Christian Eibl, once said to me that he really likes the fact that I wear my lederhosen to work, too. Worn with a jacket they really work well in the office. And he also wanted to wear his lederhosen more often and in everday life – not just at weddings and village fairs. Which is why we initated LederhosenDonnerstag. And I think what we're doing is that we're giving people who would usually not dare to wear lederhosen during the week a good opportunity to do so. And then, when somebody on the street asks: „Hey, how come you're wearing lederhosen?", then you can say: „Today is LederhosenDonnerstag." (laughs) The success really took us by surprise. And I think one of the reasons it was so successful is that it wasn't some company's marketing gag. It was just two dorks who put on lederhosen every Thursday and had fun doing so (laughs).* →

WORDRAP WITH STEFAN WIMMER:

1741 or 2019?
2019.

My masterpiece?
A pair of short, handmade lederhosen.

What I'll pass on to the tenth generation:
Craftsmanship and skill.

The biggest misconception about lederhosen?
That you can only wear them on special occasions.

L.L. / ***Mr. Wimmer, is there a clear line that divides everyday traditional costume and traditional costume for special occasions?***
S.W. / *There has been a lot of change in that particular area in the past years. Traditional costume has become much less complicated – and I'm sure Lederhosen-Donnerstag had its part in that. Nowadays you can wear a traditional jacket with lederhosen or jeans.*
G.K. / *And that's the cool thing: you can mix and match in both directions. I can wear a festive jacket with jeans or lederhosen with a polo shirt – it all works. I really, really like that. And on LederhosenDonnerstag it's not about owning handmade deerskin lederhosen. It's about celebrating traditional costume together. And when you're wearing traditional garb everything is simply more fun.*

„I guess the idea was so successful because LederhosenDonnerstag was not some company's marketing gag – it was just about two dorks who decided to wear lederhosen on Thursdays."

Georg Klampfer

L.L. / ***And how popular is traditional garb at the Salzburg Festival?***
S.W. / *At Jedermann it's tradition for many guests to come in traditional costume, men will even wear short lederhosen. For the opera premieres you wear long garments, a festive Dirndl dress or long lederhosen.*

"Traditional costume is much less complicated than it used to be."

Stefan Wimmer

L.L. / ***How many pairs of lederhosen do you own?***
G.K. / *I have five, but there are only two or three that I actually wear. They're the handmade ones – they simply fit the best. Once you get a proper pair of lederhosen that was tailor-made for you it simply works – at every occasion and for the rest of your life. I think lederhosen are for a man what a Chanel handbag is for a woman.*
S.W. / *I have three short pairs and a pair of long lederhosen.*

"A pair of lederhosen is to a man what a Chanel bag is to a woman."

Georg Klampfer

L.L. / ***How long does one usually have to wait for a pair of Wimmer Lederhosen?***
S.W. / *When have a pair of lederhosen made with us it usually takes about eight to nine weeks for the handmade ones. And I'd say most people can wait that long. Plus, a bit of anticipation is nice, right?*

Georg Klampfer is co-founder of LederhosenDonnerstag or LederhosenThursday. Together with Christian Eibl he has been advocating for more lederhosen in everday life and on the streets. Since 2015 the two gents from Salzburg have been organising the after-work event "Feierabendbier" where they invite guests to join them and celebrate in traditional costume in different locations around town and to thus bring the LederhosenDonnerstag to an end in style – with a cool beer or a glass of wine. They are supported by other members of the association who celebrate lederhosen as much as they do.

Stefan Wimmer is the manager of the tradition-steeped family enterprise "Wimmer schneidert". The company was founded in 1741 – and today they still make high-quality, tailor-made traditional garb in their original production site in Schleedorf. In the city of Salzburg their products can be purchased at Rochushof. Individuality, quality, and a regional focus are the company's main values and its goal is to make traditional costume not just "bearable" in the 21st century. It's all about making favourite pieces that perfectly accentuate the wearer's style.

© Foto: Georg Klampfer

STAMMHAUS SCHLEEDORF

Dorf 96, 5205 Schleedorf
Tel. +43 6216 / 6562

Opening hours:
Mon – Fri 8 am – noon and 1 pm – 6 pm
Sat 8 am – noon

SHOP SALZBURG

Rochusgasse 6, 5020 Salzburg
Tel: +43 662 / 8240 80

Mon – Fri 9.30 am – 6 pm
Sat 9 am – 12.30 pm

lebensfreude@wimmertracht.at, www.wimmertracht.at

SCHMECKT ALLEN,
DENEN NICHT ALLES
SCHMECKT.
Einfach leben
SEIT 1601
TRUMER
PILS
PREMIUM CLASSIC
ZERTIFIZIERTE
SLOW
BREWING
SPITZENQUALITÄT
Einfach leben!
TRUMER.AT

ALTSTADT
SALZBURG
www.salzburg-altstadt.at
hand
kopf
werk
03.05.
bis 15.11.

KOPFARBEIT

Stylish work

Christian Sturmayr im Gespräch

A talk with Christian Sturmayr

© Foto: Styling by Sturmayr Coiffeure - Stefan Dokoupil

dt. / Seit 101 Jahren steht der Name Sturmayr für Coiffeurkunst auf höchstem Niveau. Was 1918 als kleiner Friseur in Seekirchen am Wallersee begann, ist mit Sturmayr Coiffeure heute eine Branchengröße mit Salons in vier Bundesländern. Einer, der wesentlich zu diesem Erfolg beigetragen hat, ist Christian Sturmayr. Im La Loupe-Interview verrät der 35-Jährige, wie sich Frisuren im Allgemeinen und der Friseurberuf im Speziellen verändert haben und warum man sich vom Schlagwort „praktische Frisur“ verabschieden sollte.

L.L. / **Herr Sturmayr, beim Friseurberuf ist auch die Beratung sehr wichtig. Wie gehen Sie in der Regel vor?**
C.S. / Der Großteil meiner Kunden sind Stammkunden. Wenn ich aber einen Neukunden habe, dann versuche ich, die Informationen, die ich brauche – also das, was der Kunde will – so umfassend und rasch wie möglich herauszufinden. Den Kunden richtig wahrzunehmen, ist dabei ganz wichtig. Wir sind ein Dienstleistungsunternehmen, zentral ist also erst die Kundenzufriedenheit. In einem nächsten Schritt vermittle ich dem Kunden dann über eine professionelle Beratung das, was ich für ihn oder sie im Sinn hätte.

L.L. / **Gibt es auch Kundenwünsche, die nicht umsetzbar sind?**
C.S. / Ja, das gibt es. Die Gründe dafür sind ganz unterschiedlich. Manchmal sind einfach die Gegebenheiten nicht passend und meistens verstehen das die Kunden auch. Aber was Wünsche und Vorstellungen betrifft, ist der deutschsprachige Raum in meinem Metier generell speziell. Man hört ganz oft: Ich hätte gerne eine praktische Frisur. Im internationalen Vergleich – egal, in welchem Land man ist – hört man das eigentlich nie. Wir laufen ja auch nicht alle in Jogginghose herum, nur weil es praktisch ist. Man kann die Wirkung eines Menschen mit einer schönen, gepflegten Frisur durchaus gezielt steuern.

„Im deutschsprachigen Raum hört man oft: Ich hätte gerne eine praktische Frisur."

L.L. / **Ist der Beruf heute schwieriger als früher, gerade in Hinblick auf Social Media?**
C.S. / Ich finde, dass es heute eher einfacher ist. Die Kunden wissen meist, was sie wollen. Wichtig dabei ist, eine kundenorientierte Beratung zu bieten. Man muss konkret sagen, ob die Frisuren oder Farben auf dem Instagrambild überhaupt umsetzbar sind, wie sie möglich sind und welcher Aufwand dahintersteckt. Was oft vergessen wird, ist, dass der Hauptteil der Friseurkosten auf die Mitarbeiterstunden entfallen. Der Friseurberuf ist ein Handwerk, und das hat eben seinen Preis. Beim Friseur zahle ich dafür, dass sich jemand exklusiv für mich Zeit nimmt. →

„Heute ist bei einem Friseurbesuch auch der Erlebnisfaktor wichtig."

„Radikale Lösungen mache ich im Regelfall nicht."

L.L. / **Gibt es allgemeine Tipps, mit denen man immer gepflegt ausschaut, auch, wenn man es nicht zum Friseur schafft?**

C.S. / Da tue ich mir ehrlich gesagt etwas schwer. Nicht regelmäßig zum Friseur zu gehen ist für mich vergleichbar damit, als würde ich mir nicht regelmäßig die Zähne putzen. Für mich ist das eine Ideologie – man sollte es sich wert sein, gepflegt auszusehen und damit auch selbstbewusst auftreten zu können. Aber um auf die Frage zurückzukommen: Gepflegtes Haar ist entscheidend. Einmal in der Woche sollte man eine Packung machen, einen Conditioner nach jeder Wäsche. Shampoo ist nur zum Reinigen da, das pflegt nicht.

Christian Sturmayr ist gemeinsam mit seinem Vater Fred Sturmayr der Kopf von Sturmayr Coiffeure, die in vier Bundesländern vertreten sind – in Wien, Oberösterreich, Tirol und in Salzburg. Sturmayr Coiffeure wurde 1918 als kleiner Friseursalon in Seekirchen im Salzburger Flachgau gegründet. Christian Sturmayr ist seit sieben Jahren Haar-Stylist bei den Fashion Weeks in London, Paris, New York, Mailand und Berlin, wo er bei über 300 Haute-Couture-Shows von internationalen Designern mitwirkte. Der Salzburger frisierte Celebrities wie Paris Hilton, Liz Hurley oder Katy Perry und wird regelmässig für Grossevents wie den Opernball oder den Life Ball gebucht.

L.L. / **Sie sind viel international unterwegs. Wie macht man Trends alltagstauglich?**

C.S. / Das ist eigentlich ganz einfach, weil es so viele Trendfacetten gibt. Im Zuge der Beratung merkt man schnell, wie aufgeschlossen jemand ist. Meiner persönlichen Philosophie folgend bin ich kein Fan von radikalen Lösungen. Also nicht von ganz lang auf ganz kurz. Außer, es ist ausdrücklich gewünscht. Aber meistens arbeite ich mich Schritt für Schritt dorthin. Wichtig ist für mich als Friseur, dass ich in dem Moment, in dem die Kundin den Salon betritt, schon das Endergebnis vor meinem geistigen Auge sehe und gleichzeitig überlege, wie ich die Kundin dorthin bringen könnte – zu einem individuell an sie angepassten Ergebnis.

L.L. / **Spielt das Alter auch eine Rolle?**

C.S. / Ich habe Kunden, die mit Mitte 70 unglaublich offen und modern eingestellt sind. Und ich habe sehr konservative 20-jährige Kunden. Ich glaube, man sollte da nicht in

Schubladen denken. Die Bandbreite ist da enorm. Ich denke lieber in Facetten. Das ist auch das Schöne.

L.L. / **Und was trägt Frau bei den Festspielen?**
C.S. / Bei den Festspielen sieht man wahnsinnig tolle Roben und hochwertigen Schmuck. Aber bei den Haaren ist durchaus Luft nach oben. Grundsätzlich gibt es bei den Festspielfrisuren viele Facetten, nur ganz strenge Frisuren trägt man nicht mehr. Es ist grundsätzlich alles etwas weicher, etwas femininer. Wir machen den Damen gerne Frisuren, die sie schon tragen können, wenn sie vorab gemütlich an einem See etwas essen gehen und dann anschließend bei den Festspielen glänzen.

„Wir laufen ja auch nicht alle in Jogginghose herum, nur, weil es praktisch ist.“

STURMAYR COIFFEURE

Hanuschplatz 1, 5020 Salzburg

Tel. +43 662 / 8422 11

sturmayr@sturmayr.at, www.sturmayr.at

STURMAYR COIFFEURE

Rudolfskai | Makartplatz | Alpenstrasse
Wals | Europark | Eugendorf
Bad Vigaun | Altenmarkt

© Foto: Styling by Sturmayr Coiffeure - Stefan Dokoupil

© Foto: Styling by Sturmayr Coiffeure - Stefan Dokoupil

"In the German-speaking region you often hear: I'd like a practical hairstyle."

engl. / For 101 years the name Sturmayr has been standing for highest-quality hairstyling. What started out at a small hairdressers' shop in Seekirchen am Wallersee has grown to be an industry leader with salons in four provinces. And one person who has made a significant contribution to this success, is Christian Sturmayr. In his interview with La Loupe the 35-year-old told us how hairstyles in general and the job of a hairdresser in particular have changed and why it's time to say goodbye to the term "practical hairstyle".

L.L. / ***Mr. Sturmayr, for hairdressers giving customers the right advice is key. What's you usual approach here?***
C.S. / *Most of my clients are regulars. But when I get a new client I try to get all the information I need – i.e. what the client wants – as quickly and comprehensively as possible. Getting a good feel for the customers is what counts here. We are a service provider and so our customers' happiness is paramount. In the next step I try to provide the customer with professional advice and tell them what I think would work best for them.*

"Nowadays a trip to the hairdressers' should have a certain wow factor."

L.L. / ***Do customers sometimes want the impossible?***
C.S. / *Yes, absolutely. And the reasons for this are varied. Sometimes the circumstances simply don't work and the customers usually get that. But, as far as wishes and ideas are concerned, the German-speaking region is rather special for my profession. There's one thing you hear quite often: I'd like a practical hairstyle. And when you look at other countries – no matter which, really – you virtually never hear that. We don't walk around the streets in sweatpants simply because they're practical. I think that the effect that a person with a beautiful, well-groomed hairstyle has can certainly be influenced.*

"I don't usually do radical solutions."

L.L. / ***Would you say the job has become more difficult, particularly with respect to social media and their influence?***
C.S. / *I actually think it's become easier. The clients usually know what they want. And what's important is to provide the kind of advice that's tailored to the customer in question. It's important to say whether that cut or colour from the instagram post can be realised, how it can be done and what kind of effort it takes. What people often forget is that the main part of a haircut's cost is due to staff costs. The job of hairdresser is a craft and that has its price. When I go to the hairdresser's I pay for someone to make time just for me.* →

© Foto: Styling by Sturmayr Coiffeure - Stefan Dokoupil

L.L. / ***Do you have tips for people who want to always look well-groomed, even if they've not managed to see a hairdresser?***
C.S. / *Honestly, I find that difficult to do. For me not going to the hairdressers' regularly is like not brushing one's teeth regularly. It's an ideology – you should feel like you're worth it, like you deserve to look groomed and thus present yourself with self confidence. But, to return to your question: well-nourished hair is decisive. One should apply a hair pack once a week, use conditioner after every wash. Shampoo is only there to clean, not to nourish.*

"We don't run around in sweat pants all day simply because they're practical, do we?"

L.L. / ***You travel quite a bit. What is it that makes trends suitable for everyday life?***
C.S. / *That's hard to say because trends have many facets. When talking to a client you quickly notice just how open they are. Following my own personal philosophy I don't usually pick a radical solution. So, I don't just cut off very long hair. Unless that's the client's express wish. Most of the time I get there step by step though. What counts for me, as a hairdresser, is that the moment a client walks into my salon I can already see the result in front of my mind's eye and at the same time I think about how I might get the client there – to their personal, tailored result.*

L.L. / ***Would you say that age plays a role here?***
C.S. / *I have clients in their 70s who are incredibly open and have a modern attitude. And I have super conservative 20-year-olds. I really think one should avoid stereotyped thinking like that. The bandwidth really is huge. And I like to think in facets. That's the beauty of it, right?*

L.L. / ***And what's the perfect ladies' hairstyle at the Salzburg Festival?***

C.S. / *At the Festival you see stunning gowns and the finest jewellery. But when it comes to hairstyles I'd say there still is room for improvement. Generally there are many options when it comes to Festival hair, only super strict styles are no longer worn. Everything has become more soft and feminine. We like to style the ladies' hair so that they can wear it already while they're having a relaxed bite to eat at the lake and shine at the Festival after.*

Christian Sturmayr and his father Fred Sturmayr run Sturmayr Coiffeure together. The company is represented in four provinces – in Vienna, Upper Austria, Tyrol, and Salzburg. Sturmayr Coiffeure was founded in 1918 as a small salon in Seekirchen in Salzburg's Flachgau region. In the past seven years Christian Sturmayr has worked at Fashion Weeks in London, Paris, New York, Milan, and Berlin where he was active in more than 300 haute couture shows by international designers.
Born and raised in Salzburg he has styled stars like Paris Hilton, Liz Hurley, or Katy Perry and when renowned events like the Opera Ball or Life Ball come up he is always fully booked.

STURMAYR COIFFEURE

Hanuschplatz 1, 5020 Salzburg

Tel. +43 662 / 8422 11

sturmayr@sturmayr.at, www.sturmayr.at

STURMAYR COIFFEURE

Rudolfskai | Makartplatz | Alpenstrasse
Wals | Europark | Eugendorf
Bad Vigaun | Altenmarkt

PEAK PERFORMANCE

dt. / Die Erfolgsgeschichte von Peak Performance begann in einem kleinen schwedischen Bergdorf. 1986 trafen sich drei talentierte Skifahrer in Åre, im Herzen der nordschwedischen Wildnis. Sie alle trieb ein Wunsch an: Kleidung zu produzieren, die erstklassige Funktionalität mit einem schlichten und attraktiven Design verbindet. Kleidung, die nicht zu auffällig ist, aber auch nicht zu langweilig. Etwas, das sie als Outdoorfans gerne tragen möchten. Die Idee zu Peak Performance war geboren – in Åre, denn: „Where mountains touch the sky and water reaches land is where we live, create and dream."

Heute ist die schwedische Marke einer der größten Player in der Outdoorbekleidungs-Industrie. Die drei Gründer von Peak Performance holten für den Vertrieb einen vierten Mann mit ins Boot – den früheren Abfahrtsläufer Jonas Ottosson. Zum Outdoorsegment zählt auch eine hochwertige Golfkollektion. Alle Produkte von Peak Performance überzeugen mit innovativen Materialien, die einen idealen Mix aus Style und Performance ergeben. Die diesjährige Active-Wear-Linie „Vislight" steht etwa für die Kombination aus Leichtigkeit, Atmungsaktivität, Schutz und einer innovativen Designsprache mit absoluter Bewegungsfreiheit. Die Materialien passen sich perfekt an die Körperbewegungen an und trotzen dennoch jeglichen Witterungsbedingungen. So sind sie die idealen Partner für grenzenlose Outdoorabenteuer!

Das Fundament der Golfkollektion von Peak Performance bilden dünne, leichte und sehr atmungsaktive Stoffe. Die schmale Silhouette sorgt für uneingeschränkte Bewegungsfreiheit – je besser das Tragegefühl, desto besser die sportliche Leistung. Und auch das Design kommt nicht zu kurz: Die Golfkollektion überzeugt neben Komfort und Innovation mit einem anspruchsvollen Farbkonzept – der sportliche, ausgefallene Look orientiert sich dennoch am klassischen Dresscode des Golfs. In diesem Sinne: Lasset die Spiele beginnen! Der Sommer kann kommen.

PEAK PERFORMANCE STORE

Europastrasse 1, 5020 Salzburg
Tel. +43 662 / 2430 80
peak.salzburg@peakperformance.com
www.peakperformance.com

engl. / The success story behind Peak Performance began in a small Swedish mountain village. In 1986 three talented skiers met up in Åre, at the heart of the wilderness of Northern Sweden. They were all motivated by one wish: making clothing that combines first-rate functionality with simple and attractive design. Clothing that's not too flashy but also not too boring. Something that fans of the outdoors would enjoy wearing. The idea behind Peak Performance was born – in Åre, because: "where mountains touch the sky and water reaches land is where we live, create and dream."

Today the Swedish brand is one of the biggest players in the outdoor-clothing industry. The three founders of Peak Performance got a fourth man on board who would take care of marketing – the former downhill skier Jonas Ottosson. Their outdoor range also includes a high-quality golf collection. All products by Peak Performance impress with innovative materials that are used to create the perfect mix of style and performance. This year's Active Wear line "Vislight" stands for a combination of lightness, breathability, protection, and an innovative design language paired with maximum freedom of movement. The materials adjust to any movment while simultaneously braving any weather. That makes them the ideal partner for unlimited outdoor adventures!

At the basis of the Peak Performance golf collection are thin, light, and very breathable materials. The slim silhouette ensures maximum moblity – the better the wearability, the better the athletic performance. And, of course, the design aspect isn't neglected either: the golf collection impresses not only with comfort and innovation, it also sports a sophisticated colour scheme – however, the athletic, unusual look still resembles the classic golf dresscode. Well, then: let the games begin! Summer: bring it on.

PEAK PERFORMANCE STORE

Europastrasse 1, 5020 Salzburg
Tel. +43 662 / 2430 80
peak.salzburg@peakperformance.com
www.peakperformance.com

16.-20.10.2019

Jazz & The City

Salzburg

Let´s get lost!

© Foto: Seen by Streb

LOUNGE 5

Business-Netzwerk, Designausstellung & Eventlocation

business network, design exhibition & event location

dt. / In den Räumlichkeiten der LOUNGE 5 trifft lässiger Industrial Chic auf moderne Architektur. Die Mitglieder des Business-Netzwerks profitieren von einem außergewöhnlichen Umfeld, in dem anspruchsvolle Wünsche Wirklichkeit werden.

Die Hotel & Design Werkstatt im Salzburger Gusswerk wird zu LOUNGE 5. Das exklusive Netzwerk bietet seinen Mitgliedern ein breites Spektrum an Angeboten nach dem Vorbild internationaler Business Clubs. Von flexiblen Arbeitsbereichen über repräsentative Meeting Areas bis zu vollausgestatteten Seminar- und Präsentationsräumen: LOUNGE 5-Member haben im einzigartigen Ambiente der ehemaligen

Glockengießerei die Möglichkeit, flexibel zu arbeiten, Synergien untereinander zu nutzen sowie unvergessliche Events zu veranstalten. Adressaten sind neben Hotellerie und Gastronomie ab sofort auch Projektentwickler, Investoren, Entscheidungsträger sowie die gehobene Privatwirtschaft.

engl. / The premises of LOUNGE 5 perfectly combine cool industrial chic with modern architecture. The members of this business network profit from an extraordinary environment where demanding wishes are fulfilled.

Hotel & Design Werkstatt at Salzburg's Gusswerk becomes LOUNGE 5. The exclusive nework offers its members a wide range of services, much like an international business club would. From flexible workspaces to representative meeting areas and fully furbished seminar and presentation spaces: in the unique surroundings of the former bell foundry LOUNGE 5 members get to work with maximum flexibility, make use of synergies between them and host unforgettable events. Clients include hotels and restaurants as well as project developers, investors, decision makers and high-profile private enterprises.

vlnr.: Peter Zechner, Michael Mayer, Walter Raboch
© Foto: LOUNGE 5

LOUNGE 5

Söllheimer Strasse 16, Objekt 6c,
5020 Salzburg
Tel. +43 662 / 4343 00
www.lounge5.com

Öffnungszeiten:
Mo – Do 9 – 18 Uhr, Fr 9 – 15 Uhr

Opening hours:
Mon – Thu 9 am – 6 pm
Fri 9 am – 3 pm

Home & Design

Home & Design

dt. / Warum Design auch ein bisschen mit Schauspielerei zu tun hat? Darauf geht Gerald Kiska im La Loupe-Interview ein, und hat noch viele weitere spannende Antworten parat. Spannend ist auch die Idee, die hinter „The Mozart" steckt – einem Designhotel im Andräviertel, dem zwei kreative Frauen eine neue Identität gegeben haben.

engl. / How does design have anything to do with acting? In his La Loupe interview Gerald Kiska had some interesting answers to this particular question. The idea behind "The Mozart" – a design hotel in Salzburg's Andräviertel quarter – also is quite fascinating; it was two creative women who gave this place a whole new identity.

WENIG PLATZ FÜR ROUTINE

Gerald Kiska im Gespräch

A talk with Gerald Kiska

dt. / Vor knapp 30 Jahren zog Gerald Kiska aus, um seine Leidenschaft für Design professionell auszuleben. Dabei wollte er nicht der nächste Autorendesigner werden, der seine Handschrift über alles gießt. Vielmehr setzte er es sich zum Ziel, Marken zu stärken und zu positionieren. Wie exzellent ihm das bis heute gelingt, unterstreichen nicht nur über 100 internationale Preise und Auszeichnungen. Im La Loupe-Interview spricht Gerald Kiska unter anderem über die Notwendigkeit, an Grenzen zu gehen, seine Berufskrankheit und was Design mit Schauspielerei zu tun hat.

L.L. / **Seit 1990 gibt es Ihre Agentur bzw. Ihr Designbüro. Wie gehen Sie an ein Design heran, wie kann man sich diese Abläufe vorstellen? Vielleicht ein bisschen wie ein Schauspieler, der sich in eine neue Rolle einfindet?**

G.K. / Es ist tatsächlich ein bisschen wie in der Schauspielerei. Das heißt, die Routine beschränkt sich darauf, dass es in einem Theater spielt – das ist aber auch schon alles. Die Aufgabenstellung ist jedes Mal neu und anders. Dem sollte man nicht mit Routine begegnen, sondern ganz im Gegenteil mit Kreativität.

„Das Produkt ist der beste Geschichtenerzähler."

L.L. / **Wie lange dauert so ein Prozess?**

G.K. / Das hängt sehr stark von der Komplexität ab. Aber ein Projekt dauert etwa zwischen 12 und 60 Monaten.

„Wenn man nicht an die Grenzen geht, ist kein überraschendes Ergebnis möglich."

L.L. / **Stichwort Design und Redesign – was muss dabei beachtet werden?**

G.K. / Zusätzlich zum Design oder Redesign gibt es auch den Vorschlag – also das Design ohne Auftrag, sozusagen (lacht). Von daher ist der Prozess jedes Mal ein anderer. Grundsätzlich hängt es stark davon ab, wie viel schon vorgegeben ist und wie viel man in Frage stellen kann. →

„Man muss die Persönlichkeit der Marke respektieren."

Und auch, ob man mehr in Frage stellen kann als vielleicht ursprünglich gedacht. Wir versuchen immer, den Freiraum so groß wie möglich zu gestalten. Der Routine wenig Platz zu geben. Das klingt jetzt vielleicht hart, aber in der Regel kommen Kunden ja zu uns, um neue Dinge zu kreieren, und nicht, um ausschließlich in der Vergangenheit zu kramen. Wobei Vergangenheit schon wichtig ist, die Geschichte eines Produkts. Man muss wissen, wo der Kunde herkommt und wo er heute steht. Deshalb ist auch nicht alles überall machbar. Man muss die Persönlichkeit der Marke, für die man arbeitet, respektieren.

© Foto: KISKA

L.L. / **So wie bei Gasteiner Mineralwasser?**

G.K. / Genau. Wasser ist ein unsichtbares und wenig unterscheidbares Produkt, auch wenn jede Wasserquelle ein bisschen anders ist. Das Ziel ist, möglichst viel Vertrauen in die Quelle zu generieren. In Gastein steht das Quellwasser der Alpen im Vordergrund – der alpine Ursprung. Schon in der Vergangenheit wurde der Bergkristall als Synonym für die Marke zitiert. Wir haben diese Idee wieder aufgegriffen. Früher stand die industrielle Reproduktion im Vordergrund. Das heißt, man hat das Wasser einfach in eine drehrunde Flasche gegossen. Wir haben aber gesagt, ein Kristall ist nicht symmetrisch. Ein Kristall ist asymmetrisch. Damit waren wir mitten in der Technologieentwicklung. Eine Herausforderung bestand im Pressglas an sich beziehungsweise in der Tatsache, dass ein asymmetrischer Glaskörper nicht gleichmäßig abkühlt. Dabei entstehen Spannungen im Glas. Das war ein langer Weg mittels der Trial-

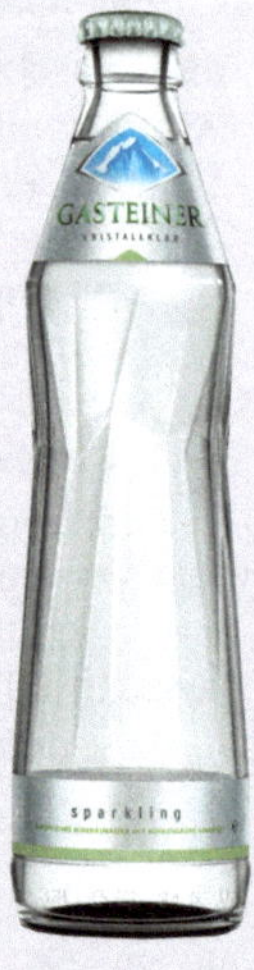

and-Error-Methode (lacht). Wir haben versucht, so viele natürliche Kristallformen wie möglich zu schaffen und gleichzeitig für die Produktion so wenig Probleme wie möglich zu generieren. Beim Bau der Modelle haben wir uns dann mit der Glasproduktion abgestimmt und um Millimeter gefeilscht, um das natürliche Kristallgefühl zu erhalten und die Kosten zugleich im Rahmen zu halten. Das zeigt, dass wir auch bei einem vermeintlich einfachen Produkt wie einer Glasflasche an die Grenzen gehen wollen, weil sonst kein überraschendes Ergebnis möglich ist.

L.L. / **Mineralwasser ist ein Alltagsprodukt. Wann hat Design den Schritt in den Alltag gemacht?**
G.K. / Heute geht es um das Erzählen von Geschichten. Marken sind dabei Ausdruck von Geschichten. Wann ist eine Marke eine Marke? Wenn Ihnen zum Begriff eine Geschichte einfällt. Design kann dieses Schreiben von Geschichten unterstützen, zum Ausdruck bringen und transparent machen. Das Produkt ist der beste Kommunikator dieser Geschichte, weil es am längsten bei Ihnen bleibt. Somit ist das Produkt der beste Geschichtenerzähler. Und je authentischer die Geschichte ist, je besser Sie sich daran erinnern können, umso leichter fällt die Entscheidung für eine Marke.

WORDRAP MIT GERALD KISKA

Auf … kann ich bei meiner Arbeit nicht verzichten.
Auf den Austausch mit meinen Kollegen.

Form follows function?
Das war schon tot, als ich studiert habe.

Was kann durch Design nicht transportiert werden?
Man kann ziemlich alles über Design transportieren.

… bräuchte mal ein neues Design.
Da gibt es eine lange Liste.

… ist für mich perfekt!
Berufskrankheit: nahezu nichts.

L.L. / **Erzählen Sie den Kunden auch noch etwas über Ihre Marke?**
G.K. / Wir fragen ab, was andere über das jeweilige Unternehmen denken. Dafür haben wir vor 15 Jahren mit Research begonnen – heute haben wir ein eigenes Team, das rausgeht und das Fremdbild abfragt. Mittlerweile haben viele Unternehmen eine gewisse Distanz zu ihren Kunden entwickelt. Wir versuchen bewusst, uns da wieder näher heranzurobben und abzufragen, wie denn die Firma, die Marke, wirklich gesehen wird. Für uns ist das ein wertvoller Faktor, um Geschichten besser erzählen zu können. →

© Foto: KISKA

Die Karriere von Gerald Kiska begann 1990 als Ein-Mann-Betrieb. Heute arbeiten im gleichnamigen Designbüro in Anif bei Salzburg 230 Mitarbeiter aus 35 verschiedenen Staaten. KISKA ist damit eines der größten eigentümergeführten Studios Europas. Das Produktportfolio des Unternehmens umfasst die Gestaltung von Produkten, Produktumgebungen und Produktkommunikation sowie die strategische Beratung. Berühmt wurde Gerald Kiska durch seine Arbeiten für den Motorradhersteller KTM, für den er unter anderem das berühmte Orange kreierte.

L.L. / **Ist Design heute noch Luxus?**

G.K. / Design ist ein Schlachtfeld, dass man genau so professionell bedienen muss wie andere Faktoren der Marke. Unser Dienstleistungsangebot geht ja mittlerweile weit über das Produkt hinaus und hat sich auch in Richtung Kommunikation entwickelt. Für die meisten unserer Kunden sind wir auch für die Kommunikationsarbeit zuständig. Wer kann schließlich besser über ein Produkt sprechen als der, der es designt hat?

L.L. / **Müssen Sie Ihren Kunden Ihre Designs manchmal erklären?**

G.K. / (lacht) Voltaire hat einmal sinngemäß gesagt: „Jedes Ding, das eine Erklärung braucht, ist die Erklärung nicht wert." Beim Design ist es genau das gleiche.

L.L. / **Stichwort Design als Hilfsmittel: Wie gehen Sie an dieses Thema heran?**

„Salzburg ist als Marke authentisch."

G.K. / Wir wollten Hilfsmitteln wie Prothesen einen erkennbaren Wert geben, und damit auch den Träger stolz machen. Das ist ein sehr sensitives Geschäft. Was uns stolz macht, variiert in der individuellen Wahrnehmung stark. Nachdem eine Prothese etwas ist, dass man anstelle eines Körperteils trägt und nicht am Körper, ist die Befindlichkeiten eine ganz andere als beispielsweise bei einem Kleidungsstück. Da muss man die Variante anbieten, die tatsächlich die persönlichen Bedürfnisse trifft. Da kann man nicht einfach alles über einen Kamm scheren. Wir haben einen Baukasten entwickelt, aus dem man seine persönliche Prothese gestalten kann, die dann auch auf das eigene Wertempfinden abgestimmt ist. Die Akzeptanz wird für den Träger dadurch leichter und das Selbstwertgefühl wird gestärkt, weil der Träger selbst Herr der Gestaltung ist und mitbeeinflussen kann, wie viel er nach außen tragen möchte.

L.L. / **Wie würden Sie in der Designsprache Salzburg beschreiben?**
G.K. / Ich würde sagen, Salzburg ist als Marke authentisch. Und alles andere als modern. Das muss es aber auch nicht sein. Salzburg verkauft sich über etwas anderes als Modernität und ich denke, so ist das auch glaubhaft.

L.L. / **Wie „designed" ist Ihr Leben?**
G.K. / Naja, man kann dem Beruf nicht entrinnen. Ich betrachte alles, was ich für mich selbst kaufe, mit den Augen eines Designers – das ist eine Berufskrankheit, die bekommt man nicht weg. Insofern ist man natürlich schon etwas wählerischer mit den Dingen, mit denen man sich umgibt. Lieber weniger und davon das Richtige als mehr vom Falschen (lacht). Ja, das ist eine Berufskrankheit. Ich kann nicht einfach irgendeinen Sessel kaufen, das geht einfach nicht (lacht).

KISKA GMBH
St. Leonharder Strasse 4, 5081 Anif
Tel. +43 6246 / 7348 80
office@kiska.com, www.kiska.com

engl. / A little under 30 years ago Gerald Kiska went off to follow his passion for design on a professional level. In doing so, however, his aim was not to become the next freelance designer to pour his own handwriting over everything. His goal was to strengthen and position brands. And just how excellently he has been doing so is not just underlined by more than 100 international honours and awards. In his interview with La Loupe Gerald Kiska spoke about the necessity of testing boundaries, his occupational disease, what design and acting have in common, and much more. →

© Foto: KISKA

L.L. / **Your agency and design studio has been around since 1990. What is your approach to a new design, how can we envision this process? Maybe you're a bit like an actor who adjusts to his new role?**

"The product is the best storyteller."

G.K. / *I'd say it really is a bit like acting. Meaning that the only routine thing about it is the location – the theatre – and that's about it. Every single time the task is new and different. So, you can't meet that with a routine process, quite the contrary – you need creativity.*

"When you don't push your boundaries you can never reach a surprising effect."

L.L. / **How long does such a process take?**

G.K. / *That would depend very much on the complexity. But usually a project takes between 12 and 60 months.*

L.L. / **Now, think keyword design and redesign – what do you need to keep in mind here?**

G.K. / *The process is different every single time. Generally speaking it all depends on what's already there and how much you can question. And also if you might be able to question more than originally thought. We always try to create as much freedom as possible and not leave any space for routine. That may sound tough, but normally our clients come to us because they want to create new things and not because all they want to do is rummage around in the past. Of course, the past is important, a product's history. It's im-*

portant to know where the customer comes from and where they stand today. Which is why not everything is feasible everyhwere. You need to respect the personality of the brand you work for.

L.L. / ***Just like with Gasteiner mineral water?***

G.K. / *Precisely. Water is an invisible product that's hard to discern, even if every single water source is a little different. The goal is to generate as much trust as possible in the source. In Gastein the focus lies on spring water from the Alps – the alpine origin. And in the past the rock crystal was already used as a synonym for this brand. We went back to that idea. In former times industrial reproduction was paramount. Which means that the water was filled in round bottles. But we said, a crystal is never symmetrical. A crystal is asymmetrical. Which is how we ended up deep inside technology development. One challenge was the pressed glass itself and the fact that an asymmetrical body of glass doesn't cool down evenly. Which leads to tension in the glass. So, in the end it was a long road and a lot of trial and error (laughs). We tried to create as many natural crystaline shapes as possible while creating as few problems for production as possible. When making the models we coordinated with the glass production and haggled over every millimetre in order to reach a natural crystal-like feel while still keeping the costs manageable. This goes to show that even when it's about a seemingly simple product like a glass bottle we test the boundaries because otherwise there can never be a surprising result.*

WORDRAP WITH GERALD KISKA

I can't do without .... at work.

The exchange of ideas with my colleagues.

Form follows function?

That was already dead when I was in uni.

What can not be transported via design?

I'd say you can transport just about anything through design.

...could use a new design.

There is a long list.

...is perfect for me!

My occupational disease: next to nothing.

L.L. / ***Mineral water is an everyday product. When did design make it into everyday life?***

G.K. / *Today it's all about telling stories. And brands are a way of expressing stories. When is a brand a brand? When the term makes you think of a story. Design can support that process of writing stories, express it and make it transparent.* →

The product itself is the best communicator of this story because it is what sticks with you the longest. Which also makes the product the best storyteller. And the more authentic the story, the better you'll be able to remember it and the easier you'll find it to decide on a brand.

"You have to respect the brand's personality."

L.L. / **Do you tell your customers about their brand, too?**
G.K. / *We look at what others think of the respective brand. In order to do so we started doing research 15 years ago and today we have a whole team that goes out and looks at the external image. Many companies have established a certain distance between themselves and their customers. And what we try to do, consciously, is to gradually come closer and ask what the actual perception of the company and the brand is like. That's an extremely valuable factor for us when it comes to telling their story better.*

"Salzburg as a brand is authentic."

L.L. / **Would you say that nowadays design still is a luxury?**
G.K. / *Design is a battlefield that needs to be worked just as professionally as other factors that make up a brand. Meanwhile our range of services goes way beyond the products and has developed in the direction of communication. For most of our clients we do communication, too. Because who could speak about a product better than the person who designed it?*

L.L. / **Do you sometimes feel like you need to explain your designs to your clients?**
G.K. / *(laughs) Speaking in Voltaire's words (more or less): "If it needs an explanation, it's not worth explaining."*

L.L. / **Design as an aid: what's your approach to this topic?**
G.K. / *We wanted to lend aids like prostheses a discernible value and make their wearers proud in the process. It's a very sensitive business. What makes us proud varies very much, depending on our individual perception. Since a prosthesis is something you wear instead of a limb and not just on your body, the feeling is very different from that of a piece of clothing, for example. So you really need to offer an option that actually meets the personal needs. You can't just go for the one-size-fits-all approach. We have developed a*

Gerald Kiska's career started in 1990 as a one-man-show. Today the eponymous design studio in Anif near Salzburg has 230 members of staff from 35 different countries. That makes KISKA one of the largest studios in Europe that's still led my its owner. The company's product portfolio comprises product and brand design & product communication as well as strategic consultation. Among the things that made Gerald Kiska famous was his work for the motorcycle manufacturer KTM for whom he designed the famous orange colour and much more.

construction kit where everyone can design their own prosthesis that matches their own values. That makes it easier to accept for the wearer und strengthens their self confidence because they themselves were in charge of design and they had an influence on how visible it will be towards the outside world.

L.L. / **How would you describe Salzburg's design language?**

G.K. / I'd say that Salzburg as a brand is authentic. And anything but modern. But it doesn't have to be. Salzburg sells through something other than modernity and I think that it's believable that way.

L.L. / **How "designed" is your life?**

G.K. / Well, you can't really escape your own profession. Everything I buy for myself I look at with a designer's eye – that's an occupational disease you can never really cure. In that sense I am, of course, a little more picky about the things I surround myself with. I prefer having less but the right kind rather than more of the wrong kind (laugs). Yes, it's an occupational disease. I can't just buy some random chair, I just can't (laughs).

© Foto: KISKA

KISKA GMBH

St. Leonharder Strasse 4, 5081 Anif
Tel. +43 6246 / 7348 80
office@kiska.com, www.kiska.com

BY NATURE AND KNOPP

MODERN MOZART

Ein Gespräch mit Martina Toifl und Pia Clodi

A talk with Martina Toifl und Pia Clodi

dt. / Wenn eine Hotel- und eine Design-Lady, beide mit Liebe zu Kunst und Fotografie, gemeinsame Sache machen, kann nur etwas Besonderes dabei herauskommen. Im neuen Boutiqehotel The Mozart im Andräviertel verschmilzt die Epoche der Klassik charmant und stilsicher mit dem 21. Jahrhundert zu einem Wohlfühl- und Inspirationsreich. Hoteldirektorin Martina Toifl und Designerin Pia Clodi geben im La Loupe-Interview Einblicke in ihr neuestes Projekt, ihren Zugang zu Mozart und die Dramaturgie hinter den 32 Zimmern.

L.L. / **Frau Toifl, aus welchen Beweggründen entstand das Hotel The Mozart?**

M.T. / Der für die Franz-Josef-Straße charakteristische Altbau, in dem sich das The Mozart befindet, stammt aus der Zeit der Jahrhundertwende und wurde seit den 1950er-Jahren als Hotel Mozart geführt. Es war in Familienbesitz und die Eigentümerfamilie hat beschlossen, das Haus zu verkaufen. Glück für uns! Wir haben den laufenden Betrieb Anfang 2018 übernommen und uns war gleich klar, dass dieses Haus viel Potenzial hat; nun, nach einer viermonatigen Renovierungsphase, erstrahlt es im neuen Glanz. So viel wir aber auch neu gemacht haben – vom französischen Vollholzboden bis zur Stuckdecke – so selbstverständlich haben auch antike Stücke ihren neuen Platz im Haus gefunden.

„Wir verstehen uns als ein individuelles Stück Salzburg."

Martina Toifl

„Kunst ist immer ein Fenster in eine andere Welt – in die Welt von jemanden, der anderes oder anders sieht als man selbst."

Pia Clodi

L.L. / **Inwiefern spielen die Stadt Salzburg, der Gast und das Design zusammen? Was darf man erwarten?**

P.C. / Martina und ich haben als Design-Duo beim Projekt „Townhouse Nora" der von Martina gegründeten Heym Collections erstmals zusammengearbeitet.

M.T. / Meine Liebe zum Design und Einrichten hat in Pia eine gute Ergänzung gefunden. Für das Townhouse haben wir vor drei Jahren gemeinsam die Einrichtung, Ausstattung →

© Foto: Theresa Pewal

und Wände als Gesamtkonzept geplant und umgesetzt: Ich wollte die Stadt ins Townhouse holen und Pia hat dafür die „Salzburg Edition" entworfen. Die Bilder an den Wänden erzählen die Geschichte der Stadt, die man draußen entdecken kann. Das kommt irrsinnig gut an. Die Gäste finden die Fotografien auch in unserem Cityguide und auf Postkarten, und nehmen so ihr Stück Kunst aus Salzburg mit nach Hause.

L.L. / **Welche Designphilosophie verfolgen Sie mit The Mozart? Retro, zeitgenössisch, modern?**

P.C. / Unseren Stil beschreiben viele als persönlich, britisch inspiriert und charakterstark, wobei das Haus und seine Geschichte für uns die Richtung vorgegeben hat. Im The Mozart sind die stilbildenden Elemente antike Möbel, erstklassige Stoffe und stimmige Farben.
So kommt auch unser Motto „A modern classic" zustande.

M.T. / Die Lower Bar, das Herzstück unseres Frühstücksbuffets, ist zum Beispiel ein alter Apothekerschrank.
Man soll sich hier geborgen fühlen, gleichzeitig darf es etwas spezieller sein als zuhause. Und man kann auch die Annehmlichkeiten des 21. Jahrhunderts genießen: Klimaanlage, Smart-TV und großartige Boxspringbetten.

„Man muss einfach in allen Zimmern gewesen sein, um alles gesehen zu haben."

Martina Toifl

„Kommt man als Gast wieder, entdeckt man immer einen anderen Teil der Story."

Pia Clodi

L.L. / **Was verstehen Sie unter einem Boutiquehotel? Was braucht ein Boutiquehotel? Was macht es aus?**

M.T. / Wir verstehen uns als ein individuelles Stück Salzburg und möchten uns auf das Wesentliche des Gastgebens konzentrieren: einen herzlichen Empfang und persönlichen Umgang mit unseren Gästen.

WORDRAP MIT MARTINA TOIFL & PIA CLODI

Lieblings-Möbelstück im Haus/Hotel?
Die Lower Bar – der Apothekerschrank.

Oberfläche schafft Geborgenheit?
Oberfläche muss echt sein. Von Nachahmungen umgeben, fühlt man sich nicht geborgen.

Zimmer #... sollte man vorreservieren?
Die Suite. Und Zimmer 103.

Salzburg, Mozart und ...
... eine Entdeckungsreise.

Das mache ich als Erstes, wenn ich nach Hause komme ...
... die Fenster auf.

Zu gleich spürt man in der Einrichtung des Hauses unsere Liebe zu Details, zur Kunst und zu Mozart.

P.C. / Boutique heißt für uns charaktervoll. In diesem Sinne haben wir mit verschiedenen Künstlern zum Thema Mozart gearbeitet – von Zeichnungen bis hin zu einem musikalisch inspirierten Spiegel. Für uns ergibt sich durch die Kunst ein anderer Blick auf die Dinge. Fotografie durfte dabei natürlich auch nicht fehlen. Für die besondere Atmosphäre in den 32 Zimmern sorgen Bilder, die als Gesamtkunstwerk eine dramaturgische Geschichte ergeben. Diese erzählen wir in unserem Buch „Mozart – kissed by the Muse". Kommt man als Gast wieder, entdeckt man wahrscheinlich jeweils einen anderen Teil der Story.

M.T. / Man muss einfach in allen Zimmern gewesen sein, um alles gesehen zu haben (lacht).

L.L. / **Stadthotel bedeutet ein reges Kommen und Gehen. Wie wahren Sie Ihren persönlichen Stil?**

M.T. / Die Zimmer haben ein klassisches Design, aber durch die Verbindung mit den Jugendstilelementen oder mit den Thonet-Stühlen ist sofort der Konnex zu Österreich da. Das Heimische, Regionale ist uns sehr wichtig – auch bei der Kulinarik. Unser Frühstück besteht großteils aus regionalen Produkten, zum Beispiel bieten wir täglich frische Smoothies und Müslis an.

L.L. / **Welche Rolle spielt Mozart als Person?**

P.C. / Mozart hat einmal gesagt: Die Musik kommt nicht aus den Noten, sondern aus der Stille dazwischen. Das ist ein sehr starkes Bild und war mein Ausgangspunkt für das →

© Foto: Pia Clodi

„Der Gast soll sich geborgen fühlen, gleichzeitig darf es etwas spezieller sein als zuhause."

Martina Toifl

„Der künstlerische Prozess ist ein spielerischer."

Pia Clodi

Kunstprojekt „Mozart – kissed by the Muse". In dieser fotografischen Einfühlung für 32 Zimmer, Bar und Bistro geht es um den künstlerischen Schaffensprozess. Dieser ist ein spielerischer. Nachdem mich persönlich die Figur der Muse seit einigen Jahren sehr beschäftigt hat, spielt sie eine wesentliche Rolle. Das Zwiegespräch des Künstlers mit seiner Muse steht sinnbildlich für die Dialektik, die in Mozarts Kompositionen überall zu finden ist.

L.L. / **Was soll der Gast „mitnehmen"?**

M.T. / Wir wollen mit The Mozart einen Ort anbieten, wo man sich aufgehoben und wohlfühlt, aber auch inspiriert wird – nicht nur Hotelgäste aus aller Welt, sondern auch die Salzburger, die in Bar und Bistro unseres Hauses herzlich willkommen sind.

P.C. / Ein Platz für lebendigen Austausch und Begegnung – bei einem guten Glas Wein (lacht).

Pia Clodi reiste als Fotografin mit ihrem Label Peaches & Mint um die Welt, bis Martina Toifl sie 2017 als Designerin und Creative Director für Heym Collections engagierte. Ihre Liebe zur analogen Fotografie zieht sich dabei nach wie vor als roter Faden durch ihre Arbeiten. Ihr Anspruch an das The Mozart-Remake war es, Design und Kunst in zeitloser Eleganz zu verbinden.

Martina Toifl ist Gründerin der Heym Collections, einer Salzburger Hospitality Brand. Nach dem Remake und Rebranding des nunmehr als Boutiquehotel geführten „The Mozart – a modern classic" heisst sie mit ihrem Team Gäste aus aller Welt willkommen.

THE MOZART

Franz-Josef-Strasse 27, 5020 Salzburg

Tel. +43 662 / 8722 74

stay@themozarthotel.com, www.themozarthotel.com

© Foto: Theresa Pewal

engl. / When a hotel and a design lady, both with a penchant for art and photography, decide to work together, the result can only be one thing: very special. The new boutique hotel The Mozart in Salzburg's Andräviertel quarter combines elements from the classical era and the 21st century in a charming and stylish fashion, thus creating a space of comfort and inspiration. In their interview with La Loupe, hotel director Martina Toifl and designer Pia Clodi divulge details about their latest project, their approach to Mozart, and the dramatic composition of 32 rooms.

"We see ourselves as an individual piece of Salzburg."

Martina Toifl

"Art always is a window into a different world – the world of a person who sees things differently than you do."

Pia Clodi

L.L. / ***Ms. Toifl, how did the hotel The Mozart come to be?***
M.T. / *The old building with its style that is so characteristic for Franz-Josef-Strasse, where it is located, dates back to the turn of the century and it was run as Hotel Mozart since the 1950s. It was family-owned until – luck for us – the family of owners decided to sell the house. We took over running →*

© Foto: Pia Clodi

operations in early 2018 and immediately realised just how much potential the house has; now, after a four-month renovation period, the house shines in new lustre. There are a lot of new things we put in there – from French wooden floors to stucco ceilings – but of course quite a few antique pieces also found a new place in the house.

L.L. / ***What sort of interaction is there between the city of Salzburg, the guest, and the design? What's to expect?***
P.C. / *Martina and I first worked as a design-duo on the project "Townhouse Nora" by the Heyn Collections that Martina founded.*
M.T. / *My passion for design and interior is complemented perfectly by Pia. Three years ago we conceived and realised the furnishing, features, and walls as a comprehensive concept at the Townhouse: I wanted to bring the city into the Townhouse and Pia designed the "Salzburg Edition" for it; the pictures on the walls tell the city's story which can be discovered outside. That concept is extremely popular. The guests can also find the photographs on our city-guide and postcards and so, when they go home, they take a piece of art from Salzburg with them.*

"You simply need to have been to every single room to have seen it all."

Martina Toifl

L.L. / ***What's the design philosophy behind The Mozart? Retro, contemporary, modern?***
P.C. / *We describe our style as personal, inspired by British design, and with a strong character – the house and its history itself pointed us in the right direction. At The Mozart the items that contribute most to its individual style are antique pieces of furniture, finest fabrics, and harmonious colour schemes. That's how our motto "A modern classic" was conceived, too.*
M.T. / *The Lower Bar, the heart of our breakfast buffet, for instance, is an old apothecary's cabinet.*

The space is supposed to make you feel comfortable while still being a little more special than your own home. And, of course, you can also enjoy all the comforts of the 21st century: AC, smart TV, and amazing box-spring beds.

L.L. / **What does the term boutique hotel mean to you? What does a hotel need to deserve the name boutique hotel?**
M.T. / *We see ourselves as an individual piece of Salzburg and we want to focus on the essentials of our job as hosts: a warm welcome, and personal interacation with our guests. At the same time the house's interior design speaks of a passion for details, for art, and for Mozart.*
P.C. / *To us boutique means full of character. Which is why we worked on the topic of Mozart together with several artists – from drawings to a music-inspired mirror. We think that art inspires a different perspective of things. So photography was a must. The 32 rooms all feature photographs that, taken together, make up a complete work of art that tells its own story. A story we also tell in our book "Mozart – kissed by the Muse". Whenever a guest returns they probably get to discover yet another element of the story.*
M.T. / *You simply need to have been in all the rooms to have seen it all (laughs).*

"When guests return they get to discover a different part of the story."

Pia Clodi

L.L. / **A city hotel means a lot of hustle and bustle. How do you preserve your personal style?**
M.T. / *The rooms have a classical design, and because of the connection with art nouveau elements or the Thonet chairs, there immediately is an Austrian flair to it. The original, the regional was important to us – also when it comes to food. Our breakfast is made up of mostly regional produts, and we offer fresh smoothies and mueslis every day.* →

WORDRAP MIT MARTINA TOIFL & PIA CLODI

Favourite piece of furniture in the house/ hotel?
The Lower Bar – the apothecary's cabinet.

Surfaces creates comfort?
A surface needs to be real. No-one feels at home surrounded by fakes.

We'd recommend booking room #... in advance.
The suite. And room 103.

Salzburg, Mozart and ...
... a voyage of discovery.

The first thing I do when I get home...
...I open the windows.

L.L. / **What role does Mozart as a person play?**

P.C. / *Mozart himself said it once: music is not made up of notes, but the silence in between. That's a really strong image and it was the starting point for the art project "Mozart – kissed by the muse". This photographic concept for 32 rooms, bar, and bistro is all about the process of artistic creation. Which, in this case, is very playful. And since the personal figure of the muse has been on my mind for several years, it plays a decisive role. The dialogue of the artist and his muse symbolises a kind of dialectic that can be found all over Mozart's compositions.*

As a photographer Pia Clodi traveled the world with her own label Peaches & Mint – until 2017 when Martina Toifl hired her as desinger and creative director for Heym Collections. Her passion for analogue photography is visible in all of her work – like a red thread. Her claim in the The Mozart-remake was to combine design and art in timeless elegance.

Martina Toifl is the founder of Heym Collections, a Salzburg-based hospitality brand. After the remake and rebranding, the hotel "The Mozart – a modern classic", which is now led as a boutique hotel, welcomes guests from all over the world.

"We want the guest to feel comfortable while at the same time giving them something that is a little more special than their own home."

Martina Toifl

"The artistic process is playful."

Pia Clodi

L.L. / **What do you want the guest to "take away"?**

M.T. / *With The Mozart we want to offer guests a place where they can feel comfortable and at home but also inspired – and that does not just go for hotel guests from all over the world but also for people from Salzburg who are very welcome in our bar and bistro.*

P.C. / *A space for lively exchange and encounters – with a good glass of wine (laughs).*

THE MOZART

Franz-Josef-Strasse 27, 5020 Salzburg
Tel. +43 662 / 8722 74
stay@themozarthotel.com, www.themozarthotel.com

NEU in
SALZBURG
Mi. bis Fr.: 10–18 Uhr
Sa.: 10–14 Uhr
und nach Vereinbarung
largilla.at

l'argilla
FLIESE
ALTE MATTSEER STRASSE 14A | 5020 SALZBURG | WWW.LARGILLA.AT

Kunst & Kultur

Arts & Culture

dt. / Wenn Damen in edlen Roben und Herren im noblen Zwirn über die Staatsbrücke flanieren, ist es wieder soweit: Die Salzburger Festspiele machen die Stadt jedes Jahr zur Bühne der Welt. Doch auch abseits des berühmten Festivals gibt es viel zu erleben – etwa, wenn jazzige Klänge beim „Jazz & The City" Gäste und Einheimische zum Tanzen bringen.

engl. / When women in elegant gowns and men in snazzy suits leisurely cross Staatsbrücke bridge the time has come once more: each year Salzburg Festival turns the city into a stage for the world. However, there is much more to experience than the famous festival – the jazzy sounds of "Jazz & The City" where guests and locals alike are inspired to dance, for example.

© Foto: SF Ruthwalz

EIN MYTHISCH-SCHÖNER FESTSPIELSOMMER

A mythical and beautiful festival summer

199 Aufführungen in 43 Tagen an 16 Spielstätten – die Salzburger Festspiele sind das ultimative Sommerevent

199 performances in 43 days and 16 locations – Salzburg Festival is the ultimate summer event.

Kunst & Kultur

dt. / Von 20. Juli bis 31. August 2019 steht die gesamte Stadt Salzburg wieder im Zeichen der weltberühmten Festspiele. Bereits zum 99. Mal werden Opern, Schauspiel und Konzerte Menschen aus der ganzen Welt verzaubern – dieses Jahr unter anderem mit Mozart, Strauss, Händel und den Wiener Philharmonikern. Festspielfreunde dürfen sich unter anderem auf fünf Opern- und vier Schauspielneuinszenierungen sowie auf die „Jedermann"-Wiederaufnahme freuen.

© Foto: matthiashorn

Intendant Markus Hinterhäuser wirft beim diesjährigen Festspielsommer einen neuen Blick auf die antiken Mythen. Den Auftakt bildet mit der offiziellen Eröffnungspremiere am 27. Juli Mozarts „Idomeneo" vor der spektakulären Kulisse der Felsenreitschule. Für die Inszenierung zeichnet das Regie-Dirigentenduo Peter Sellars und Teodor Currentzis verantwortlich, die 2017 bereits mit „Clemenza die Tito" das Publikum begeistern konnten.

Auch die erneute Inszenierung der „Salome" von Richard Strauss ist ein Highlight, genauso wie die Wiederaufnahme der Oper „Alcina" von Georg Friedrich Händel aus dem Programm der Pfingstfestspiele. In der Felsenreitschule werden die Wiener Philharmoniker für Begeisterung bei Musikliebhabern sorgen, genauso wie die Ouverture Spirituelle, „Orchester zu Gast" und zahlreiche Kammerkonzerte. →

Bereits Ende des Ersten Weltkriegs existierte die Idee, die jahrhundertealte Schauspieltradition in Salzburg weiterzuführen. Der Regisseur Max Reinhardt, der Dichter Hugo von Hofmannsthal und der Komponist Richard Strauss waren schliesslich Jahre später die Gründerväter der Salzburger Festspiele, die sie mit der Erstaufführung des „Jedermann" am 22. August 1920 auf dem Domplatz aus der Taufe hoben. Die Salzburger Festspiele gelten als das weltweit bedeutendste Festival der klassischen Musik und darstellenden Kunst.

Schauspieldirektorin Bettina Hering überzeugt mit vier spannenden Neuinszenierungen, Schauspiel-Recherchen und Lesungen. Auch beim ewigen Publikumsmagneten, dem Jedermann, gibt es 2019 einige Neuerung. Unter anderem wird Valery Tscheplanowa als neue Buhlschaft über die Bühne tanzen und gemeinsam mit Jedermann Tobias Moretti am Bankett feiern. Die Wiederaufnahme von Hugo von Hofmannsthals Meisterwerk steht 14 Mal auf dem Spielplan.

Die diesjährigen Sommerfestspiele setzen mit dem Thema Mythos einen mehr als passenden Schlusspunkt unter die Überthema-Trilogie, die 2017 mit „Macht" ihren Ausgang genommen hat. Denn, wie Festspielpräsidentin Helga Rabl-Stadler in einem Interview unterstrich: „Das passt sehr gut zu den Festspielen, die selbst ein Mythos sind."

KARTENBÜRO SALZBURGER FESTSPIELE

Herbert-von-Karajan-Platz 11, 5020 Salzburg
Tel. +43 662 / 8045 500, Fax +43 662 / 8045 555
info@salzburgfestival.at, www.salzburgerfestspiele.at

Öffnungszeiten:
Mo – Fr 10 – 12.30 Uhr und 13 – 16.30 Uhr

engl. / From July 20 to August 31, 2019 the city of Salzburg will once again be all about its famous festival. For the 99th time operas, theatre productions, and concerts will enchant guests from all over the world – this year's highlights will include Mozart, Strauss, Handel, the Vienna Philharmonic Orchestra, and much more. Fans of the festival can also look forward to five new opera and four new theatre productions as well as a revival of "Jedermann". →

JEDERMANN

For this year's festival summer artistic director Markus Hinterhäuser decided to take a look at classical mythology. The official opening premiere on July 27 will be Mozart's "Idomeneo" in front of the spectacular backdrop of Felsenreitschule. The director/conductor duo Peter Sellars and Teodor Currentzis are responsible for this production; back in 2017 they already amazed the audience with "Clemenza di Tito".

The new production of Richard Strauss' "Salome" is another highlight, just like Georg Frederick Handel's opera "Alcina" which will be taken from the Pentecost festival programme. The Vienna Philharmonic Orchestra will doubtlessly amaze music lovers at Felsenreitschule, just like the Ouverture Spirituelle, "Orchester zu Gast" (= a concert series with different guest orchestras), and numerous chamber concerts.

Theatre director Bettina Hering impresses with exciting new productions, actors' talks, and lectures. The all-time audience's favourite Jedermann will also see some new elements in 2019. The new Buhlschaft, Valery Tscheplanowa, will dance across the stage and feast at the banquet with Jedermann Tobias Moretti. The revival of Hugo von Hoffmannsthal's masterpiece will be played 14 times.

With the topic of myths at the focus, this summer's festival also represents a fitting endpoint to the trilogy of overarching topics that started in 2017 with "Power". The festival's president, Helga Rabl-Stadler, pointed out in an interview: "It goes well with the festival which is a myth in itself."

Kunst & Kultur

The idea of continuing the century-old acting tradition in Salzburg already existed at the end of the World War I. Years later the director Max Reinhardt, the poet Hugo von Hoffmannsthal, and the composer Richard Strauss ended up becoming the Salzburg Festival's founding fathers; it launched with the first performance of "Jedermann" on 22 August 1920 on Salzburg's Domplatz. The Salzburg Festival is considered the world's most significant festival for classical music and performing arts.

TICKET OFFICE SALZBURG FESTIVAL

Herbert-von-Karajan-Platz 11, 5020 Salzburg
Tel. +43 662 / 8045 500, Fax +43 662 / 8045 555
info@salzburgfestival.at, www.salzburgfestival.at

Opening hours:
Mon – Fri 10 am – 12.30 pm and 1 pm – 4.30 pm

JAZZ & THE CITY

16. – 20. OKTOBER 2019

dt. / Ab 16. Oktober heißt es wieder: Jazz is back in town! Jazz & The City ist längst zum herbstlichen Fixpunkt im Salzburger Kulturkalender avanciert und begeistert Jahr für Jahr rund 25.000 Besucher.

Bespielt wird die gesamte Altstadt – von Kirchen über Galerien und Konzerthäusern bis hin zu Bars oder Weinkellern. Neben dem musikalischen Genuss zeigt sich dadurch auch die Vielfalt Salzburgs. Auf der Suche nach neuen Klängen trifft man auf Gleichgesinnte und genießt eine lockere und ungezwungene Festivalatmosphäre, guten Wein und vor allem erstklassige Musik zwischen Jazz, Worldmusic und elektronischen Clubsounds. Heimische und internationale Jazzgrößen geben sich die Klinke in die Hand, und auch Nachwuchskünstlern wird eine Bühne geboten. So wundert es nicht, dass Jazz & The City in Insiderkreisen als Österreichs lässigstes Jazzfestival gehandelt wird.

Weitere Informationen: www.salzburgjazz.com

engl. / Starting on October 16 the motto in the city of Salzburg will once again be: Jazz is back in town! Jazz & The City has become by now a fixed point in Salzburg's cultural calendar and every autumn it delights around 25,000 guests.

The entire old town – from churches to galleries and concert halls to bars and wine cellars – becomes a stage. Aside from providing excellent musical entertainment the city of Salzburg also gets to show off its diversity.

Kunst & Kultur

While looking for new tunes you can meet like-minded people and enjoy a relaxed and casual festival atmosphere, excellent wine, and – above all – first-class jazz, world music, and electronic club sounds. Local and international jazz stars stream on and off stage and young artists also get plenty of attention. So, it really is no wonder that Jazz & The City is already known to insiders as Austria's coolest jazz festival.

For more information, see: www.salzburgjazz.com

5 Tage – 30 Bühnen – 70 Konzerte – freier Eintritt!
5 days – 30 stages – 70 concerts – free of charge!

UND ES HAT KLICK GEMACHT

And then it clicked

dt. / Von Atlanta bis Zürich: Fotografie ist ein wichtiges Medium für Menschen auf der ganzen Welt. Ihre schier endlosen Möglichkeiten macht die Leica Galerie und Boutique sichtbar.

Von Contemporary Art bis New Talents. Von Architektur bis Aktfotografie. Moderne Ikonen und ewige Klassiker. Die Leica Galerie und Boutique stellt ausgewählte Stücke der historischen und zeitgenössischen Fotografie in den Fokus. 2006 kaufte der Österreicher Andreas Kaufmann die deutsche Traditionsmarke auf und entwickelte das Portfolio weiter.

© Foto: Richard Schabetsberger

Mittlerweile ist die Leica Galerie, die es weltweit 24 Mal gibt, auch international zu einem wichtigen Begegnungsort für Fotografie avanciert. Zusätzlich stellt die Galerie in Salzburg regelmäßig an verschiedenen Locations aus, etwa im Schloss Arenberg, im Hotel Sacher oder im Foyer der Festspielhäuser.

Kunst & Kultur

engl. / From Atlanta to Zurich: Photography is an important medium for people everywhere in the world. And Leica Gallery and Boutique now show all its seemingly endless possibilities.

From Contemporary Art to New Talents. From Architecture to Nude Photography. Modern icons and eternal classics. Leica Gallery and Boutique focuses on selected pieces from historic and contemporary photography. In 2006 Andreas Kaufmann from Austria bought the traditional German brand and started to further develop its portfolio. Today Leica Gallery has 24 locations all over the world and it has become an internationally renowned meeting point for photography. In addition to that the gallery in Salzburg regularly exhibits in different locations – among them are Arenberg castle, Hotel Sacher, or the Salzburg Festival Halls' foyers.

Das Wissen um die Kunst der Fotografie wird regelmässig in Workshops weitergegeben.

Knowledge about the art of photography is regularly passed on during workshops.

LEICA GALERIE UND BOUTIQUE

Gaisbergstrasse 12, 5020 Salzburg
Tel. +43 662 / 8752 54
salzburg@leica-galerie.com, www.leica-galerie-salzburg.com

Öffnungszeiten:
Di – Fr 14 – 18 Uhr, Sa 10 – 14 Uhr
Opening hours:
Tue – Fri 2 pm – 6 pm, Sat 10 am – 2 pm

Kulinarik & Genuss

Cuisine & Delights

dt. / Sterne finden sich in Salzburg nicht nur am Firmament, sondern auch auf dem Teller – im übertragenen Sinne, versteht sich. Die Sterneköche Andreas Senn und Christian Geisler ließen La Loupe beim Interview in die Kochtöpfe blicken. Und Haubenkoch Andreas Döllerer verrät unter anderem, was für ihn die wichtigste Zutat in allen Gerichten ist.

engl. / Not just the sky above Salzburg is full of stars – its plates are, too; figuratively speaking, of course. In their interview with La Loupe, star-chefs Andreas Senn and Christian Geisler let us take a peek into their pots. And star chef Andreas Döllerer told us what the most important ingredient in all dishes is.

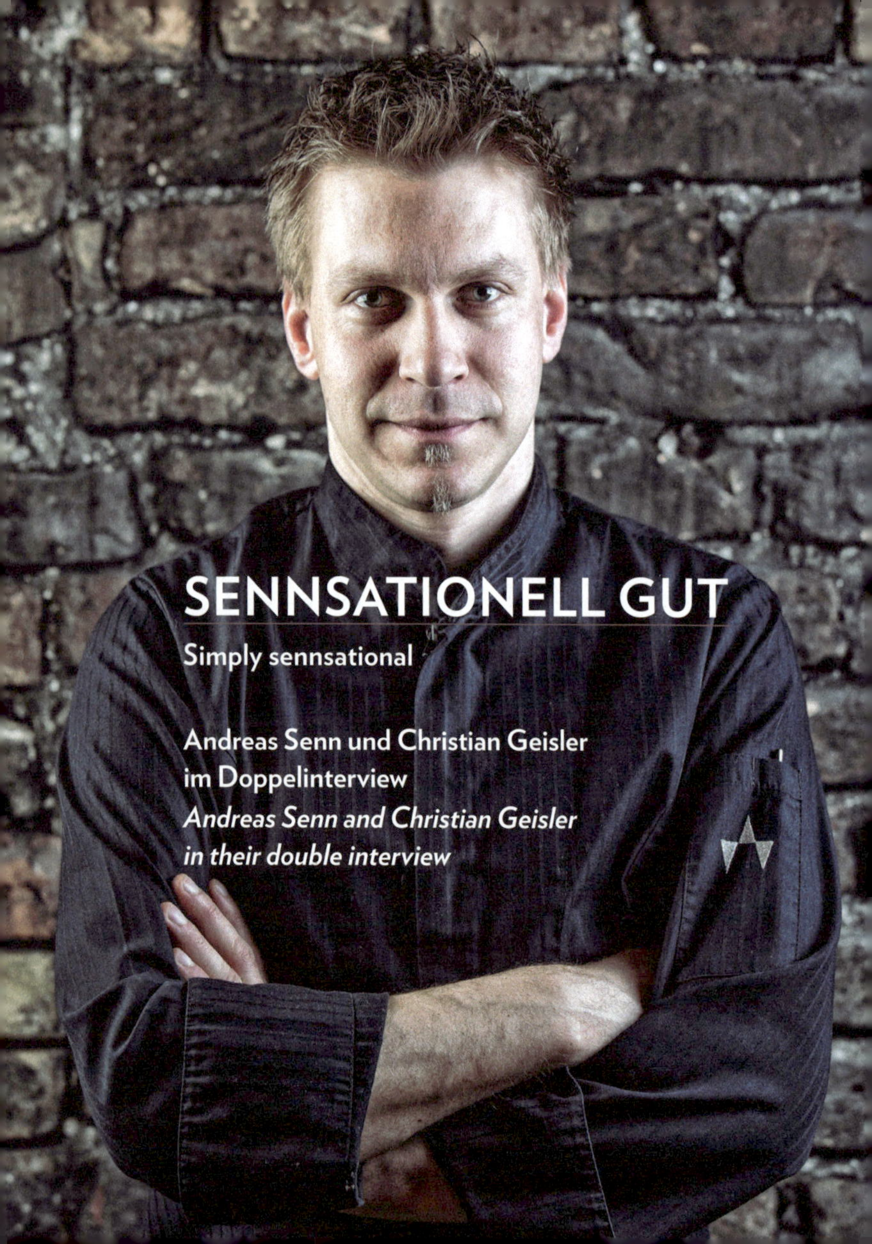

SENNSATIONELL GUT

Simply sennsational

Andreas Senn und Christian Geisler
im Doppelinterview

*Andreas Senn and Christian Geisler
in their double interview*

dt. / Andreas Senn zählt erst 39 Jahre, sein Restaurant bereits zwei Michelin-Sterne. Das liegt an seinem außergewöhnlichen Können, das er bereits in heimischen und internationalen Häusern unter Beweis gestellt hat – vom Hangar 7 bis zur Heimatliebe in Kitzbühel. Es liegt aber auch an seinem Kompagnon Christian Geisler, 34 Jahre jung, gebürtiger Salzburger und ebenfalls Sternekoch. Im La Loupe-Doppelinterview sprechen die beiden Ausnahmeköche über den Weg abseits ausgetrampelter Pfade, Schwellenangst in der Spitzengastronomie und über das Tüfteln bis zur Perfektion.

L.L. / **SENNS.Restaurant! Ein Name, ein Statement? Für was steht SENNS.Restaurant?**

A.S. / Früher, als Jugendlicher, hatte ich immer den Plan, mich mit einem eigenen Restaurant selbstständig zu machen. Dann arbeitet man eine Zeitlang in der Gastronomie und verliert diesen Wunsch etwas aus den Augen, weil man merkt: Das kostet alles richtig viel Geld. Ich war fünf Jahre lang in Kitzbühel mit dem Restaurant Heimatliebe schon sehr erfolgreich. Nachdem es geschlossen wurde, musste ich mich neu orientieren. In dem Sommer, bevor das SENNS.Restaurant eröffnet wurde, haben wir hier im Gusswerk ein Pop-up-Restaurant gemacht, damals noch unter dem Namen Heimatliebe. Ich habe mich sofort in diese Location verliebt. Aber es war jahrelange Arbeit, bis alles genehmigt wurde, bis alle Partner mit an Bord waren. Als es dann soweit war, war mir klar, dass das Lokal ein Gesicht braucht, einen Namen. Es „das Lokal im Gusswerk“ zu nennen war für mich nie eine Option. Es braucht ein Gesicht, eine Persönlichkeit. Die Gäste sollen ja Spaß haben im Restaurant und die dürfen auch spüren, dass wir Spaß haben. Hin und wieder kommen sogar Gäste in die Küche, wenn wir gerade kochen. Erst kürzlich waren wieder ein paar da, hat Christian erzählt. →

„Entscheidend sind die richtige Qualität, die richtige Zubereitung und eine eigene Handschrift.“

Christian Geisler

„Das Wichtigste an einem Gericht sind perfekte Zutaten.“

Andreas Senn

© Fotos: SENNS. Restaurant

C.G. / Ja, das waren Berufskollegen mit einem eigenen Restaurant. Die haben mich gefragt, ob sie einen Blick in die Küche werfen dürfen, als ich gerade draußen im Service war. Wir servieren ja auch mit. Das macht die ganze Atmosphäre gleich etwas lockerer und wir können die Gerichte einfach noch etwas anders erklären.

L.L. / **Sie haben gemeinsam zwei Sterne – eine Besonderheit! Wie haben Sie beide zusammengefunden?**
A.S. / Früher haben wir im Hangar 7 zusammengearbeitet – sogar zweimal. Danach haben wir uns etwas aus den Augen verloren. Ich bin in Österreich geblieben, Christian war in der Schweiz.
C.G. / Ich war fast zehn Jahre in Restaurants in der Schweiz, in Zürich und in Zermatt. Als dann mein Kind unterwegs war, haben meine Partnerin und ich beschlossen, wieder zurückzugehen. Ich bin aus Salzburg, hier sind meine Wurzeln. So hat sich das mit dem Andi eigentlich durch Zufall ergeben. Wir haben uns getroffen, Kaffee getrunken und geratscht. Dann hat der Andi gefragt, ob ich nicht zu ihm kommen will. Da habe ich nicht lange überlegt – das ist so ein lässiges Haus! Es ist Andis Restaurant, aber ich kann mich damit sehr, sehr gut identifizieren. Und bin froh, dass ich da sein kann.
A.S. / Uns verbindet eine private Freundschaft. Und in der Küche macht jeder sein eigenes Ding, das ergänzt sich super. Das sieht man auch an den Gerichten.

„Das Ziel ist nicht, zu kopieren, sondern kopiert zu werden."

Christian Geisler

„Das grösste Problem der Sternegastronomie ist die Schwellenangst."

Andreas Senn

L.L. / **„Wer nie die ausgetrampelten Pfade verlässt, kommt nur dort an, wo andere schon waren." Diese Aussage liest man von Ihnen oft. Wo waren Sie und haben sich inspirieren lassen?**

A.S. / Die prägendste Zeit für mich waren sicher die sieben Jahre im Hangar 7. Was man da mitbekommt, mit elf verschiedenen Gastköchen im Jahr, das ist schon Wahnsinn. Der Spruch ist dadurch entstanden, dass die Gourmetrestaurants alle irgendwie gleich sind – oft sehr steif. Gott sei Dank hat sich das schon etwas geändert. Wir wollten unser Restaurant bewusst anders machen. Zum einen ist die Location keine klassische Restaurant-Location – wir haben keine Tischdecken, kein Silberbesteck. Zum anderen ist die Küche etwas frecher, moderner. Es soll einfach Spaß machen.

„Andreas und ich servieren auch – dann können wir den Gästen noch mehr über die Gerichte erzählen."

Christian Geisler

L.L. / **Welcher spezifische Geschmack unterscheidet Ihr Restaurant von anderen?**

C.G. / Ich glaube, das Ziel ist nicht, zu kopieren, sondern kopiert zu werden. Wir tüfteln ständig an Gerichten herum, probieren viel aus, auch gewisse Zubereitungsarten. Wir versuchen, nichts zu kopieren, sondern machen das, was uns selbst schmeckt. Das treiben wir dann so zur Perfektion, bis wir sagen: Das kommt jetzt auf unsere Karte.

A.S. / Das Schöne ist: Was uns schmeckt, schmeckt vielen Gästen auch (lacht).

„Zu uns kommen 18-Jährige genauso wie 70-Jährige."

Andreas Senn

L.L. / **Inwieweit verändern zwei Sterne den Geschmack?**

A.S. / Man kann davon ausgehen, dass man ein perfektes Grundprodukt vor sich hat. Generell sind das Wichtigste an einem Gericht perfekte Zutaten. Das geht beim Gemüse los, und betrifft natürlich besonders Fisch und Fleisch. Diese Qualität hat eben auch seinen Preis. Wir können Langustino kaufen, da kostet das Kilo 20 Euro. Oder wir kaufen Langustino um 120 Euro pro Kilo. Das ist ein Riesenunterschied in der Qualität. Und das schmeckt man.

C.G. / Die Qualität, die richtige Zubereitung und die eigene Handschrift, das macht es aus. →

Andreas Senn, Eigentümer und Küchenchef im Spitzenrestaurant SENNS, legte den Grundstein für seine steile Karriere bereits zu Lehrlingszeiten. Schon damals nahm er an Wettbewerben teil und erkochte sich, nach seinem Lehrabschluss mit Auszeichnung, 2003 seine erste Haube im Gault Millau. Viele weitere Auszeichnungen sollten folgen, unter anderem die als „Koch des Jahres", ausserdem mehrere Hauben und Sterne. Ab 2013 erhielt er dreimal in Folge drei Hauben von Gault Millau für seine Kreationen im Restaurant Heimatliebe Kitzbühel. 2015 konnte Andreas Senn den ersten Michelin-Stern für SENNS in Empfang nehmen, 2016 folge der zweite.

Der gebürtige Salzburger Christian Geisler war bereits in mehreren Städten als Koch erfolgreich, bevor er wieder zurück nach Salzburg ging – etwa in New York City, in Chicago, in Zürich oder Zermatt. 2014 und 2015 wurde er mit einem Stern im Guide Michelin ausgezeichnet. Seit 2018 steht er neben Andreas Senn in der Küche des Salzburger Spitzenrestaurants SENNS.

L.L. / **Geben Sie diese Geschichten auch an den Gast weiter?**

A.S. / Ja, das ist auch ein Grund, warum wir mitservieren – damit wir es den Gästen noch besser erklären können. Den Interessierten erklären wir gerne, was es mit den Zutaten auf sich hat. Warum alte Milchkuh, beispielsweise, und kein Black Angus Beef. Aber in erster Linie soll es dem Gast schmecken, der Gast soll Spaß haben und einen schönen Abend genießen. Wie, wenn er ins Theater gehen würde.

„Ich kann mich mit Andis Restaurant sehr, sehr gut identifizieren."

Christian Geisler

L.L. / **Wir haben gehört, es fliegen extra Gäste ein, um hier zu essen. Wen wollen Sie ansprechen?**

A.S. / Wir haben Gäste, die kommen extra aus Taiwan oder China, um bei uns zu essen. Für diese „Gourmettouristen" ist der Guide Michelin wahrscheinlich ausschlaggebend. Ich denke, dass uns diesbezüglich auch die drei Sterne gut tun werden, die das Amador in Wien bekommen hat. Dadurch kommen vielleicht noch mehr Gourmets zu uns nach Salzburg. Grundsätzlich haben wir aber kein klassisches Gästeklientel. Zu uns kommt der 18-Jährige mit seiner Freundin zum Geburtstagsessen genauso wie ältere Herrschaften mit 70 Jahren. Wir haben viele Stammgäste, die schon in Pension sind. Sicher ist das Preisniveau ein Thema, wir sprechen eine gewisse Schicht an. Aber auch ein 18-Jähriger kann es sich einmal im Jahr leisten – dann ist es eben ein richtiges Erlebnis. Und wir haben keinen Dresscode, es muss niemand in Anzug und Krawatte kommen.

„Wir wollten von Anfang an alles bewusst anders machen."

Andreas Senn

Bei uns muss man keine Angst haben, bei uns sollen sich

auch die jungen Leute wohlfühlen. Wir wollen diese Schwellenangst unbedingt dämmen. Ich denke, die Schwellenangst ist das größte Problem der Sternegastronomie.

L.L. / **SENNS und das englische Wort „sense" für Sinn - lassen vermuten, dass man bei Ihnen mit allen Sinnen genießen kann. Gerne möchte man sich an dieses Erlebnis lange erinnern - gibt es ein Geschmacksgedächtnis?**
C.G. / Wenn das Essen richtig gut ist, bleibt es in Erinnerung. Ich weiß wahrscheinlich mein Leben lang, wo ich das beste Barbecue gegessen hab. Die ganz guten, spezifischen Sachen, die merkt man sich.
A.S. / Ich glaube, es muss einfach Klick machen, visuell und geschmacklich. Dann bleibt es auch in Erinnerung.

SENNS.RESTAURANT

Im Gusswerk
Söllheimerstrasse 16, Objekt 6, 5020 Salzburg
Tel. +43 664 / 4540 232
info@senns.restaurant, www.senns.restaurant

© Foto: Senns Restaurant

engl. / Despite his young age of 39 years Andreas Senn's restaurant already has two Michelin stars. And that is due to his extraordinary skill which he has put to the test plenty of times in regional and international houses – from Hangar 7 to "Heimatliebe" in Kitzbühel. And it is also because of his Salzburg-born partner Christian Geisler, 34 years old, who also happens to be a star cook. In their La Loupe double interview the two extraordinary chefs speak about their path off the beaten track, "threshold fear" in top gastronomy, and about tinkering to perfection. →

© Foto: SENNS. Restaurant

L.L. / ***SENNS.Restaurant! A name, a statement? What does SENNS.Restaurant stand for?***

A.S. / *In the past, when I was in my teens, I always had a vision of opening my own restaurant. Then you work in the restaurant industry for a while and you lose sight of that wish because you realise: all of that costs a lot of money. During my five years at Heimatliebe in Kitzbühel I was quite successful. After it was closed I had to find myself again. During that summer, before SENNS was opened, I opened a pop-up restaurant here at Gusswerk, still under the name Heimatliebe. I immediately fell in love with the location. It took years of work until we had all the permits and the right partners were on board. When the time finally came I knew the restaurant would need a face, a name. Calling it the "restaurant at Gusswerk" was never an option for me. It needs a face, a personality. The guests are supposed to enjoy themselves at the restaurant and they should also see that we're having fun. Occasionally, the guests will even pay us a visit in the kitchen while we're cooking. Christian told me that only recently a few people came by and popped in.*

„What's most important is the right quality, the right preparation, and your own handwriting."

Christian Geisler

„Perfect ingredients are the most important part of a dish."

Andreas Senn

C.G. / *Yes, they were colleagues who have their own restaurant. They asked if we'd be ok with them having a look around the kitchen while I was out serving food. Yes, we also help with the serving. That makes the whole atmosphere a bit more relaxed and we can also explain the dishes a little differently.*

L.L. / ***Between you two you have two stars – that's quite unusual! How did you find each other?***

A.S. / *We used to work together at Hangar 7 – twice, even.*

After that we kind of lost sight of each other. I stayed in Austria while Christian was in Switzerland.
C.G. / *I was in restaurants in Switzerland, in Zurich and Zermatt, for almost ten years. Then, when my kid was on its way, my partner and I decided to come back to Austria. I am from Salzburg, my roots are here. And the thing with Andi was a coincidence, really. We met up and had a coffee and we chatted. Then Andi asked me if I'd like to join him. It didn't take me long for me to make up my mind – it's just such a great place! It's Andi's restaurant but I really, really identify with it. I'm really happy I get to be here.*
A.S. / *We are connected by a private friendship. And in the kitchen we each do our own things and we complement each other perfectly. Which is pretty obvious in our dishes.*

„Our goal is not to copy but to be copied."

Christian Geisler

L.L. / ***"If you never stray from the beaten path you'll only ever get to where others have already been." This is something you say a lot. Where did you go to find new inspiration?***
A.S. / *The most formative time for me were the seven years at Hangar 7. The things you learn there, with eleven different guest chefs each year, that's really crazy. And that saying came up because all gourmet restaurants are somehow the same – and often really stiff. Thankfully this has changed a bit in recent years, though. We wanted to consciously create a different kind of restaurant. For one thing the location isn't a classic restaurant location – there are no table cloths and there is no silverware. And the cuisine is more daring, more modern. It's simply supposed to be fun.*

„The single biggest problem in top gastronomy is that kind of threshold fear."

Andreas Senn

L.L. / ***What specific taste sets your restaurant apart from others?***
C.G. / *I think our goal is not to copy but to be copied. We keep playing around with our dishes, we try out many things and tinker with preparation methods. We try never to copy anything, instead we make what we like. And we keep doing this until we reach perfection and then we say: now, this can go on our menu.*
A.S. / *And the best thing is: what we like many guests like, too (laughs).* →

Andreas Senn, owner and chef de cuisine at the top restaurant SENNS, laid the foundation for his stellar career while he was still in training. Back then he constantly took part in competitions and after receiving his apprenticeship certificate (with honours), he got his first Gault Millau toque in 2003. Many other awards were to follow, among them the "chef of the year" as well as several toques and stars. Starting in 2013 he was awarded three toques by Gault Millau for his creations at Heimatliebe Kitzbühel three times in a row. In 2015 he was awarded the first Michelin-star for SENNS and in the 2016 the second one followed.

Originally from Salzburg, Christian Geisler successfully cooked in several cities before returning to his hometown – among them were New York City, Chicago, Zurich or Zermatt. In 2014 and 2015 he was honoured with one star by Guide Michelin. He has been cooking alongside Andreas Senn in Salzburg's top restaurant SENNS since 2018.

„Andreas and I do some serving, too – that way we get to tell the guests even more about the dishes."

Christian Geisler

„We have guests who are 18 and others who are in their 70s."

Andreas Senn

L.L. / ***How do two stars change the taste?***
A.S. / *You can assume that you'll always be working with the perfect base product. The most important thing about a dish are perfect ingredients. That starts with the vegetables and, of course, goes especially for fish and meat. And this kind of quality has its price. We can buy langustino for 20 euros per kilo. Or we buy the kind of langustino that costs 120 euros per kilo. There's a huge difference in quality there. And you can taste that.*
C.G. / *The quality, the right preparation, and your own handwriting, that's what it's all about.*

L.L. / ***Do you pass these stories on to your guests, too?***
A.S. / *Yes, and that's also why we do service, too – so that we can explain certain things to our guests even better. If someone's interested we're happy to tell them all about the ingredients. Why we use old dairy cow and not Black Angus Beef. But, first and foremost, we want the guest to enjoy the food, to have a good time and a lovely evening. Just like they would if they went to the theatre.*

L.L. / ***We hear there are guests who fly in to eat here. Who is your target audience?***
A.S. / *We do have guests who come from Taiwan or China to eat with us. With these "gourmet tourists" it's probably the*

Guide Michelin that brings them here. And in this respect I think the three stars that the Amador in Vienna has already, will be good for us. This way even more gourmets will find their way to Salzburg. In general, however, we don't have a classic clientele. We get 18-year-olds who take their girlfriends out for a birthday dinner or older folks of 70 years and more. We have many regulars who are already retired. Of course, the price is an issue and we therefore attract a certain kind of people. But even an 18-year-old can afford to come here once a year – and then it's sure to be quite the experience. And we don't have a dresscode, so no-one has to show up in a suit and tie. We don't want people to be hesitant about coming here, we want everyone to feel comfortable. We very much want to reduce that kind of "threshold fear". I think that threshold fear is the single biggest problem top gastronomy has.

„I can really, really identify with Andi's restaurant."

Christian Geisler

„We consciously wanted to do things differently right from the start."

Andreas Senn

L.L. / ***SENNS and the English word "sense" - makes you think that you're supposed to enjoy with all your senses here. And, of course, we want to remember this experience for as long as possible; would you say there is a taste memory?***
C.G. / *When food is really good it is also memorable. I will probably remember the best barbeque I ever had all my life. I'd say you do remember the really really good and special things.*
A.S. / *I think all it needs is a click, in terms of visual experience and taste. And if that's there you'll remember it.*

© Foto: SENNS. Restaurant

SENNS.RESTAURANT

Im Gusswerk
Söllheimerstrasse 16, Objekt 6, 5020 Salzburg
Tel. +43 664 / 4540 232
info@senns.restaurant, www.senns.restaurant

goedwinemakers

goedwinemakers.at
Wer eine kurze Geschichte hat, bemüht sich umso mehr um eine lange Zukunft.
Warum fängt ein erfolgreicher Unternehmer auf einem Weingut nochmal komplett von vorne an? Wer hat die Salzburger Bergwelt gegen die südsteirischen Weinberge eingetauscht? Und was motiviert einen waschechten Sernauberger dazu ein Goedwinemaker zu werden? Das erzählen wir Ihnen gerne bei einem Glas Wein.
Und auf goedwinemakers.at.
Sernau 29 / 8462 Gamlitz / Österreich
T +43 664 2809 600

© Fotos: Sporer

HOCHPROZENTIGER GENUSS

A most spiritual indulgence

dt. / Man kann getrost behaupten: Der Sporer ist eine echte Institution in der Mozartstadt. Seit 1903 gibt es den Familienbetrieb in der Getreidegasse – und beinahe so lange ist er In-Treffpunkt für Einheimische wie Gäste.

Die Rezeptur des berühmten Orangenpunschs stammt von Gründer Franz Sporer, die beliebte Hausmischung von Otto Sporer. Michael Sporer führt den Betrieb heute in vierter Generation und hat es sich zum Ziel gesetzt, dessen Erbe zu bewahren. Dass das hervorragend funktioniert, davon kann man sich bei einem Bummel durch die Getreidegasse überzeugen. In und vor dem kleinen Geschäft treffen sich regelmäßig Genießer aus allen Ecken der Welt, um auf das Leben anzustoßen. Und auf den Sporer, der die Tradition des Likör- und Punschhandwerks im Herzen der Altstadt hochhält.

Kulinarik & Genuss

Lohnenswert ist auch ein Abstecher in die Manufaktur, wo auf 110 Quadratmetern die Sporer-Fläschchen wiederaufgefüllt und ausgewählte Weine, Gin, Whisky sowie regionale Destillate angeboten werden.

engl. / It's safe to say that in the city of Mozart Sporer is a true institution. The family-run business on Getreidegasse was founded in 1903 and has been the place to be for locals and guests for almost as long.

The recipe for the famous orange punch dates back to the founder, Franz Sporer, the popular house mixture to Otto Sporer. Today Michael Sporer is in charge of managing the business in its fourth generation and it is his declared goal to preserve its rich heritage. A stroll through Getreidegasse will quickly prove that he's been quite successful. Epicures from all over the world congregate inside and outside the little shop to toast to life. And to Sporer, who keeps the tradition of making liqueurs and punch varieties at the heart of the old town alive. Also worth a visit: the 110 square metre manufactory where the Sporer bottles are refilled and selected wines, gin, whisky and regional spirits are on offer.

SPORER
LIKÖR- & PUNSCHMANUFAKTUR

Getreidegasse 39, 5020 Salzburg
Tel. +43 662 / 8454 31
office@sporer.at, www.sporer.at

Öffnungszeiten:
Mo – Fr 9.30 – 19 Uhr, Sa 8.30 – 17 Uhr
Opening hours:
Mon – Fri 9.30 am – 7 pm, Sat 8.30 am – 5 pm

DIE MANUFAKTUR SPORER

Michael Walz Gasse 22, 5020 Salzburg
Tel. + 43 662 / 4350 43
office@sporer.at, www.sporer.at

Öffnungszeiten:
Mo – Fr 9 – 12.30 Uhr, 14 – 18 Uhr
Samstag, Sonn- und Feiertag geschlossen
Opening hours:
Mon – Fri 9 am – 12.30 pm, 2 pm – 6 pm
Closed on Saturdays, Sundays and public holidays

LIEBESERKLÄRUNG

Declaration of Love

Josef Sigl 8. am offenen Gärbottich / *Josef Sigl the 8th by an open fermentation vat* © Foto: Trumer Privatbrauerei

dt. / Wir lieben Bier und leben eine zukunftsweisende Bierkultur. Eine Kultur für Menschen, die bewusst genießen und gutes Bier als hochwertiges Lebensmittel wertschätzen. Mit Zuversicht, Mut und Haltung setzen wir uns für eine lebenswerte Zukunft ein. Dafür kreieren wir Biere mit Charakter, die einzigartig schmecken und gut tun. Biere, die eine Liebeserklärung an das Leben sind, die einen spüren lassen, dass man da ist. Hier und jetzt.

Die in Obertrum am See ansässige Trumer Privatbrauerei wurde 1601 gegründet und befindet sich seit 1775 im Besitz der Familie Sigl. Seit 2013 leitet Josef C. Sigl das Familienunternehmen in achter Generation. Trumer gilt in Österreich als Pilsspezialist: das Trumer Pils, dessen Qualität laufend durch höchste internationale Auszeichnungen bestätigt wird, ist im Laufe der Firmengeschichte zum Fahnenträger der Brauerei avanciert.

Mit Haltung

Als unabhängige, inhabergeführte Privatbrauerei nehmen wir uns die Freiheit, Bier nach unseren eigenen Wertvorstellungen zu brauen: offen vergoren, mit mehr Zeit nach der Philosophie von Slow Brewing und mit bestem Naturhopfen. Seit acht Generationen.

Einfach leben

Wir von Trumer möchten inspirieren und Mut machen. In unserem Einfach Leben Podcast auf einfachleben.com lassen wir daher außergewöhnliche Menschen zu Wort kommen, die unsere Werte teilen und das Glas halb voll sehen.

Slow Brewing Gütesiegel / *Slow Brewing seal of quality*

www.trumer.at

TRUMER PRIVATBRAUEREI

Brauhausgasse 2, 5162 Obertrum am See
beer@trumer.at, www.trumer.at

engl. / We love beer and we live a future-oriented beer culture. A culture for people who enjoy consciously and who appreciate good beer as a high-quality drink. We stand for a more liveable future – with optimisim, courage, and attitude. And that's why we create beers that have character, that have unique taste and foster well-being. Beers that are a declaration of love to life, that make you feel you're here. Right here and right now.

Trumer Gärkeller / *Trumer's fermentation cellar* © Foto: Trumer Privatbrauerei

With Attitude

As an independent, owner-managed private brewery we take the liberty of making beer according to our own standards: fermented in open vats, with plenty of time, following the Slow Brewing philosophy, and using only the best natural hops. For eight generations.

Just Live

We from Trumer want to inspire and instil courage. In our "Einfach Leben" podcast on einfachleben.com we give extraordinary people, who share our values and who also see the glass as half full, speak up.*

**einfach leben = just live*

www.trumer.at

The Trumer private brewery is located in Obertrum am See; it was founded in 1601 and has been family-owned by the Sigl family since 1775. In 2013 Josef C. Sigl took over management of the family business in its eigth generation. Trumer is an Austrian specialist for pilsner beers: the quality of Trumer Pils is constantly confirmed by the highest international awards and over the course of the company's history it has become the brewery's flagship.

TRUMER PRIVATBRAUEREI

Brauhausgasse 2, 5162 Obertrum am See
beer@trumer.at, www.trumer.at

© Foto: Lukas Kirchgasser

EIN GUTES BAUCHGEFÜHL

That gut instinct

Andreas Döllerer im Gespräch

A talk with Andreas Döllerer

dt. / Entscheidungen trifft Andreas Döllerer meist aus dem Bauch heraus. Überhaupt ist der Haubenkoch aus Golling bei Salzburg bodenständig geblieben. Wenn er für seine Familie kocht, kommen gerne klassische Gerichte auf den Tisch.

Für die Gäste in seinem preisgekrönten Genießerrestaurant zaubert er den Geschmack seiner Heimat auf die Teller. Mit La Loupe hat Andreas Döllerer über seine „Alpine Cuisine" gesprochen, über die Bedeutung von Familie und die wichtigste Zutat in allen Gerichten.

L.L. / **Herr Döllerer, den Grundstein für Döllerers Genusswelten legte Ihr Großvater. Was ist die Geschichte Ihres Betriebs?**

A.D. / Unser Haus ist schon seit 1909 sowohl Wirtshaus als auch Metzgerei. Die Produktion unserer Metzgerei ist mittlerweile ausgelagert, aber nach wie vor werden die Spezialitäten nach den alten Rezepten meines Onkels hergestellt und in unserer Feinen Kost angeboten.
In den 1960-er und 70er-Jahren war Golling ein florierender Tourismusort – die ersten deutschen Pauschaltouristen haben hier Urlaub gemacht. Mein Vater hat sich in den frühen 1980er Jahren entschieden, mehr auf Qualität zu setzen und einen gut funktionierenden touristischen Betrieb auf ein Gourmetrestaurant umzustellen. Das war erst schwierig – es war in den 1980ern nicht üblich, von Salzburg nach Golling zum Abendessen zu fahren. Aber meine Eltern haben das durchgezogen. Beispielsweise hat mein Vater den damaligen Küchenchef von Eckart Witzigmann aus der Aubergine in München geholt. Der hat einfach grandios gekocht! Das waren die ersten kulinarischen Erfahrungen meiner Kindheit. Von 1990 bis 2004 war Bernhard Hauser Küchenchef, der hat mich persönlich sehr geprägt. Bis dahin hatte noch nie ein Familienmitglied gekocht. Ich war 2002 in einem Drei-Sterne-Restaurant angestellt, als die Frage aufkam, ob ich das Ruder in der Küche übernehmen sollte. Schließlich habe ich dann 2004, mit 24 Jahren, die Küche übernommen. →

WORDRAP MIT ANDREAS DÖLLERER

Der Geschmack von ....
erinnert mich an Heimat!
Schwarzbeernocken.

Wenn ich nicht koche...
trinke ich gerne ein Glas Wein.

Das habe ich zuletzt in der Küche gelernt:
Man lernt dauernd.

Küche laut oder leise?
Leise.

© Foto: Jörg Lehmann Döllerer

Die letzten 15 Jahre sind extrem schnell vergangen, waren aber auch sehr erfolgreich. Mit 2008 haben wir den Schritt in Richtung Cuisine Alpine vollzogen, seit 2010 ist es eine geschützte Marke. Wir haben dieses ganzheitliche Konzept als erster Betrieb im Alpenraum umgesetzt, mittlerweile machen das viele Kollegen. Ich finde es toll, weil wir gemeinsam stärker sind. Ob sich die Alpenküche per se durchsetzt, weiß ich nicht. Aber das ist einfach unsere Art, zu kochen – mit den Zutaten, die wir vor der Haustüre haben. Wir arbeiten weiter an dieser Idee, gehen raus in die Natur, holen Wurzeln, Beeren und alles, was wir so finden. Das Spannende ist auch, dass viele Sachen selten oder noch nie in der Küche verwendet wurden. Mit einer Enzianwurzel wurde beispielsweise bis jetzt hauptsächlich Schnaps gemacht. Wir kreieren aber laufend komplette Gerichte damit. Das gibt es bei uns neben Klassikern wie Saibling aus dem Bluntautal oder Wild aus dem Salzburger Land. Wild und Milchprodukte sind für mich auch die beiden Signature-Produkte unserer Region.

„Ich fahre nicht nach Japan, um dann in Golling japanisch zu kochen."

L.L. / **Wurde der Sinn für Genuss innerhalb der Familie weitergegeben, etwa wie ein Handwerk?**

A.D. / Meine Eltern und Großeltern haben zwar nie selbst gekocht, aber insbesondere meine Eltern sind bis heute echte Genussmenschen. Das haben sie uns Kindern auch vorgelebt. Ich war etwa drei oder vier Jahre alt, als ich das erste Mal in Frankreich in einem Drei-Sterne-Restaurant gegessen habe. Ich denke, es spielt schon eine große Rolle, ob man Kinder von klein auf zu solchen Genuss-Spots mitnimmt. Wir waren mit unseren drei Söhnen schon ganz oft in tollen Restaurants. Ich hoffe, dass sie das auch prägen wird. Ob sie dann ebenfalls Koch werden – keine Ahnung. Aber ich hoffe, sie werden auch Genussmenschen. Das ist für mich das Entscheidende.

Kulinarik & Genuss

L.L. / **Wie wichtig ist Familie?**

A.D. / Sehr wichtig. In unserer Familie hilft jeder mit und wir halten zusammen. Der Erfolg, den wir haben, ist der Erfolg unserer Familie, nicht nur der meiner Person. Ich denke, es funktioniert auch so gut, weil der Betrieb vor allem durch den Weinhandel eine ganz andere Größe bekommen und jeder seinen eigenen Bereich hat, in dem er frei arbeiten kann. Man trifft sich dann von Zeit zu Zeit und tauscht sich aus. Aber jeder hat eine eigene Entscheidungsgewalt. Ich denke, dass ist das Erfolgsgeheimnis unserer Familie.

L.L. / **Sie bieten Kochbücher, Kochkurse, den Chef's Table – lassen Sie gerne hinter die Kulissen blicken?**

A.D. / Unsere Familie ist der Gastgeber und wir schätzen den Kontakt zu unseren Gästen. Wir haben da keine Berührungsängste. Ich denke, das macht auch den Charme des Hauses aus und unterscheidet uns von vielen Mitbewerbern – die Gäste fühlen sich in der Familie aufgehoben. Um auf die Frage zurückzukommen: Kochkurse gab es bei uns schon seit den 1980er-Jahren. Ich halte nichts davon, ein Rezept geheim zu halten. Es schmeckt auch immer anders – je nachdem, wer es kocht.

„Der Erfolg, den wir haben, ist der Erfolg unserer gesamten Familie."

© Foto: Döllerers Genusswelten

L.L. / Wenn man eines Ihrer Gerichte zuhause nachkochen möchte: Was braucht man dafür?

A.D. / Liebe! Es bringt nichts, wenn ich mich dazu zwinge, etwas zu machen. Wir haben Gäste, die unsere Rezepte bis ins letzte Detail nachkochen – bis zum Gletschersand. Die machen das dann auch mit Liebe und haben eine Riesenfreude damit. Das ist großartig! Genau dafür machen wir die Kochbücher.

„Wir kochen einfach gerne mit dem, was wir vor der Haustüre haben."

L.L. / Was gibt es bei einem Familienessen der Familie Döllerer?

A.D. / Da gibt es meistens ganz klassische Gerichte. Oft auch Speisen, die ich als Kind zu Festtagen bekommen habe – etwa Kalbsnierenbraten oder Kalbsbraten. Das haben wir eigentlich fast immer bekommen, fällt mir auf (lacht).

L.L. / Wie gehen Sie mit Foodtrends um?

A.D. / Die Frage ist, was man als Trend sieht. Ich besuche die Länder, die im Trend liegen, gerne – etwa Peru, Skandinavien oder Japan.

© Foto: Döllerers Genusswelten

Das heißt aber nicht, dass das per se eine Rolle in unserer Küche spielt. Ich weiß gerne Bescheid, was rund um die Welt in den Restaurants passiert. Ich fahre aber nicht nach Japan, um dann bei uns zuhause japanisch zu kochen. Es gibt manchmal Einflüsse – etwa welchen Respekt die Japaner vorm Ursprungsprodukt haben – da kann man viel lernen. Und das versuche ich, auch meinen Mitarbeitern weiterzugeben. Ein Trend wie die molekulare Küche, die in den Nullerjahren stark vertreten war, hat heute noch Einfluss in der Küche. Das ist aber bei Weitem nicht bei allen Trends so. Wichtig ist, dass man nicht jedem Trend nachläuft, sondern bei seiner eigenen Philosophie bleibt. Man kann open minded sein und die eigene Küche immer wieder weiterentwickeln. Aber man sollte nicht sagen: Alle kochen vegan, jetzt machen wir auch ein veganes Menü. Das wäre für mich etwas zu einfach.

„Ich halte nichts davon, ein Rezept geheim zu halten."

Andreas Döllerer wächst als „Wirtshauskind" im elterlichen Betrieb auf. Nach seiner Kochausbildung und mehreren Aufenthalten im Ausland kehrt er in den Familienbetrieb zurück, wo er die Cuisine Alpine etabliert. Inspirationen und Zutaten für seine vielfach preisgekrönte Küche erhält er aus den Salzburger Alpen. Als Teil seines Erfolgs sieht der 40-Jährige die mehr als 20-köpfige Familie, die die Döllerers Genusswelten repräsentiert. Zu den Genusswelten der Familie Döllerer zählen das Geniesserrestaurant, das urige Wirtshaus – bereits seit über 100 Jahren Treffpunkt für Jung und Alt – der Feinkostladen Feine Kost und das Geniesserhotel. Der Feinkostladen ist Dreh- und Angelpunkt für ausgezeichnete Fleischspezialitäten, die nach alten Familienrezepten hergestellt und an der Feinkosttheke angeboten werden. Das familiär geführte Vier-Sterne-Geniesserhotel ist besonders bei Gästen beliebt, die die Nähe zur Festspielstadt Salzburg schätzen, aber das gemütliche Ambiente im ländlichen Umfeld der Innenstadt vorziehen. In Döllerers Enoteca & Weinhandelshaus, vor den Toren Gollings, wählen private Weinliebhaber und Grosshandelskunden Weine, Schaumweine und Spirituosen namhafter Erzeuger aus der ganzen Welt aus.
Die Enoteca ist ein Genussreich für sich, in dem man bei mediterranen Antipasti und österreichischen Schmankerln die herrlichen Weine vor Ort verkosten kann.

L.L. / **Gibt es einen konkreten Plan, wo es in Zukunft hingehen soll?**

A.D. / Wir machen nie Pläne. Das alles hat sich in den letzten Jahren aus dem Bauch heraus entwickelt. Wir hatten keine strategischen Ziele, was wir etwa in den nächsten fünf Jahren erreichen wollen oder so. Das war nie unser Weg. →

Je größer das Unternehmen wird, desto mehr denkt man natürlich auch über solche Sachen nach. Aber ich wehre mich da eigentlich immer etwas dagegen. Ich habe mir bei allen Entscheidungen immer das Bauchgefühl erhalten. Deshalb habe ich keine Ahnung, was in 20 Jahren sein wird (lacht). Aber grundsätzlich wollen wir immer besser werden, in jedem Bereich – im Weinhandel, im Hotel, in der Küche. Aber in welche Richtung das konkret geht, da muss man einfach abwarten. In 20 Jahren werden hoffentlich schon meine Söhne kochen. Oder meine Neffen. Oder meine Nichten.

DÖLLERERS GENUSSWELTEN

Markt 56. 5440 Golling
Tel. +43 6244 / 42200
office@doellerer.at, www.doellerer.at

DÖLLERERS WEINHANDELSHAUS

Kellau 160, 5431 Kuchl
Tel. +43 6244 / 20567
weinhandel@doellerer.at, www.weinhandelshaus.at

engl. / When making decisions, Andreas Döllerer likes to listen to his gut. The gourmet chef from Golling near Salzburg has generally remained very down-to-earth. When he cooks for his family he likes to serve classic dishes. And for the guests of his award-winning Genießerrestaurant (= indulgence restaurant) he likes to capture the taste of his native region. In his talk with La Loupe, Andreas Döllerer spoke about "Alpine Cuisine", about the importance of family, and the most important ingredient in every dish.

© Foto: Jörg Lehmann Döllerer

L.L. / ***Mr. Döllerer, it was your grandfather who laid the foundation for Döllerers Genusswelten (= world of indulgence). What's the history behind your company?***

A.D. / *Our house has been an inn and a butcher shop since 1909. Nowadays the production of our meat products is outsourced, but all the specialties are still made using my uncle's old recipes and then sold at our Feine Kost. In the 1960s and 1970s Golling was a lively tourist destination – the first German package holiday tourists vacationed here. In the early 1980s my father decided to focus more on quality and turned an efficient tourism enterprise into a gourmet restaurant. That was tricky at the beginning – back in the 1980s one did not just go from Salzburg to Golling for dinner. But my parents saw it through. And to do so they got Eckart Witzigmann's chef de cuisine from Munich's Aubergine. His cooking was simply magnificient! And those were the first culinary experiences of my childhood. Between 1990 and 2004 Bernhard Hauser was chef de cuisine and he had a great influence on me. I was the first one in the family to become a cook. In 2002, when I was working in a two-star restaurant, the question of whether I'd like to take over the kitchen came up.* →

"I don't go to Japan to come back and cook Japanese in Golling."

So, in 2004, when I was 24 years old, I took over the reins in the kitchen. Those past 15 years have passed very quickly but they were also quite successful. In 2008 we took the step towards Cuisine Alpine and since 2010 the name has been a protected trademark. We were the first to realise this holistic concept in the alpine region and many of my colleagues have since followed suit. I think that's great because we're all stronger together. I don't know if alpine cuisine per se will last. But it simply is our way of cooking – with ingredients we find just outside our doors. We keep working on this idea, we keep going out into nature, collecting roots, berries, and everything else we can find. What's exciting about it is that many of the things have only rarely or never been used in the kitchen. Up until now, for example, gentian root was usually only used to make schnapps. Now we keep coming up with new complete dishes with it. That's what we serve alongside classics like the char from Bluntautal valley or game from Salzburger Land. Game and dairy products are the two signature products of our region.

"We enjoy cooking with ingredients we find just outside our door."

WORDRAP MIT ANDREAS DÖLLERER

The taste of…reminds me of home!
Schwarzbeernocken – a type of blueberry pancake..

When I'm not cooking…
I like to enjoy a glass of wine.

What did I last learn in the kitchen?
You learn all the time.

Noisy or quiet kitchen?
Quiet.

L.L. / ***Would you say that that sense for indulgence was passed down to you in your family, like a trade?***

A.D. / *While my parents and grandparents were never cooks themselves, I'd say that my parents in particular are and always have been true epicureans. I was about three or four years old when I first ate at a three-star restaurant in France. I think whether or not you take your kids to such hotspots of indulgence from the beginning on does make a big difference. We have taken our three sons to many great restaurants. And I hope that that's going to make an impact, in the long run. Whether they'll decide to become chefs themselves – that I don't know. But I do hope they'll turn into epicureans, too. If you ask me – that's what counts.*

L.L. / ***How important is family to you?***
A.D. / *Very important. In our family we all help each other and we stick together. The success we have is the success of our family, not of an individual person. And I think the only reason it's working so well is that the company has reached a certain size, particularly as a result of the wine trading, and everybody has their own area where they can work freely. From time to time we do meet up and exchange thoughts. But still, everyone makes their own decisions. I think that that's my family's secret to success.*

© Foto: Jörg Lehmann Döllerer

L.L. / ***You sell cookbooks, host cooking courses, the chef's table – do you enjoy letting people peek behind the scenes?***
A.D. / *We, our family, are the hosts and we appreciate the contact with our guests. There are no reservations there. And I think that that's what makes up the charm of our house and what sets us apart from many other competitors – with our family the guests feel at home. And, to come back to your question: we already hosted cooking classes back in the 1980s. I don't think keeping one's recipes secret is a good idea. It always tastes different anyway – depending on who's cooking.*

L.L. / ***If someone were to cook one of your dishes at home: what would they need?***
A.D. / *Passion! There's no use in forcing myself to do something. We have guests who've copied and emulated our recipes down to the smallest detail – even with the glacier sand. And they did it with a lot of passion and the process made them happy. That's amazing! And that's exactly why we write the cookbooks.*

L.L. / ***And what is usually served at a Döllerer family meal?***
A.D. / *Usually I make classic dishes. And things I myself got on holidays as a child – like roast loin of veal or roast veal. Come to think of it, that's what we almost always had (laughs).* →

Andreas Döllerer grew up an "innkeepers' boy" at his parents' inn and hotel. After his training as a chef and several stays abroad he came back to the family business where he subsequently established Cuisine Alpine. For his award-winning cuisine he draws inspiration and ingredients from Salzburg's Alps. The 40-year-old sees his more than 20-strong family which respresents Döllerers Genusswelten (= world of indulgence) as a vital part of his success. The Döllerer family's Genusswelten are made up of the Geniesserrestaurant, the rustic inn – which has been a popular meeting place for young and old for more than 100 years – the delicatessen shop Feine Kost and the Geniesser-hotel (= indulgence hotel). The delicatessen shop is the place to go for selected meat specialties that are made using old family recipes and can be purchased at the delicatessen counter. The family-run four-star Geniesserhotel is popular with guests who appreciate the vicinity to the festival city of Salzburg but prefer a comfortable, rural environment to the city's hustle and bustle. At Döllerer's Enoteca & Weinhandelshaus (the wine shop), just outside Golling, private wine lovers as well as wholesalers get to chose their favourite wines, champagnes, and spirits from renowned producers from all over the world. The Enoteca is it's own world of indulgence where Mediterranean antipasti and Austrian delicacies can be combined with a tasting of wonderful wines.

"The success we have is the entire family's success."

L.L. / **What's your approach to food trends?**

A.D. / The question here is what you see as a trend. I like visiting countries that are trendy – like Peru, Scandinavian countries, or Japan. But that does not mean they have to play a role in our kitchen. I like to know what goes on in kitchens all over the world. But I don't go to Japan to come back and cook Japanese at home. Sometimes there are influences – like the Japanese respect for the original product – and there is much to learn. And that's what I try to pass on to my members of staff. A trend like molecular cuisine, which was quite strong during the early 2000s, still influences our kitchen. But that certainly does not go for all trends. What's important is to not go chasing after every trend, but to stick to one's own philosophy. You can be open minded and keep developing your own cuisine. But I don't think it's wise to say: everyone's into vegan cooking now, so we'll make our own vegan menu, too. That would be a little too easy for me.

"I don't see why one should keep recipes secret."

L.L. / ***Are there any concrete plans for the future?***

A.D. / *We never make plans. In the past years everything has developed based on a gut instinct. There were no strategic goals; something to accomplish in the coming five years or so. That was never our path. The bigger the company the more you do think about such things, of course. But I usually refuse such notions. I have always known to stick to my gut instinct when making decisions. Which is why I have no idea where we'll be in 20 years (laughs). But, generally speaking, we want to become better in every area – wine trading, the hotel, the kitchen. However, I don't know what concrete path we'll take, we'll just have to wait and see. And in 20 years I hope that my sons will be doing the cooking. Or my nephews. Or my nieces.*

DÖLLERERS GENUSSWELTEN

Markt 56. 5440 Golling
Tel. +43 6244 / 42200
office@doellerer.at, www.doellerer.at

DÖLLERERS WEINHANDELSHAUS

Kellau 160, 5431 Kuchl
Tel. +43 6244 / 20567
weinhandel@doellerer.at, www.weinhandelshaus.at

Guide

Guide

dt. / Geschichtsträchtiges Hotel und junges Lifestyle-Konzept, gediegene Nobelboutique und bodenständiger Handwerksbetrieb, stilvolles Restaurant am Berg und gemütliche Stube in der Altstadt – in Salzburg Stadt & Land vereinen sich scheinbare Gegensätze zu einem stimmungsvollen Ganzen. Viel Freude mit Ihrem neuen La Loupe-Guide!

engl. / Historic hotel and young lifestyle concept, snazzy and elegant boutique and traditional crafts business, a stylish restaurant on the mountain and a cosy parlour in the old town – the city of Salzburg & its surrounding region know how to unite apparent opposites to form a perfect whole. Enjoy leafing through your new La Loupe guide!

Shopping & Lifestyle Guide

EIBL.

Individuelle Modeboutique am Kajetanerplatz

Shopping & Lifestyle Guide

Vom Lebensmittelgeschäft zur Modeboutique: Seit 1972 schätzen Kunden das angenehme Ambiente und die erfahrenen Mitarbeiter der Modeboutique Eibl., die stilsicher durch die liebevoll ausgesuchten Kollektionen führen. Drykorn, Filippa K., Samsøe & Samsøe, Masons, Seductive, Seidensticker und viele weitere besondere Marken für Damen und Herren dürfen hier probiert werden. Neben Kleidung führt Eibl. im angesagten Kaiviertel in Salzburg auch Handtaschen, handgemachte Babyalpakamützen, seidenweiche Fairtrade-Schals, angesagte Lesebrillen, Naturkosmetik von Be my Friend und kleine Wohnaccessoires.
Egal ob klassisch oder trendy, jung oder jung geblieben – in der Modeboutique Eibl. werden alle fündig, die Wert auf Individualität legen.

A grocery store turned fashion boutique: since it opened in 1972 the customers of Modeboutique Eibl. have always appreciated the comfortable flair and the assistance of experienced staff who lead them through the carefully chosen collection with an eye for style. Drykorn, Filippa K., Samsøe & Samsøe, Masons, Seductive, Seidensticker, and many other special brands for women and men can all be tried on here. Aside from clothing Eibl., which is located in Salzburg's hip Kaiviertel quarter, also stocks handbags, handmade baby alpaca hats, super soft fairtrade scarves, stylish reading glasses, natural cosmetics from Be my Friend, as well as small living accessories. No matter if it's classic or trendy, young or young at heart - at Modeboutique Eibl. everyone who cares about individual style will find what they're looking for.

Öffnungszeiten:
Di - Fr
10 - 18 Uhr
Sa 10 - 17 Uhr

Opening hours:
Tue - Fri
10 am - 6 pm
Sat 10 am - 5 pm

EIBL. KAJETANERPLATZ
Schanzlgasse 4, 5020 Salzburg
Tel. +43 662 / 8436 13
shop@eibl.or.at, www.eibl.or.at

KUNSTGÄRTNEREI DOLL

Shopping & Lifestyle Guide

Aufgeblüht

Wer schon einmal die geschichtsträchtige Gärtnerei im Nonntal betreten hat, weiß: Der Name Doll steht für mehr als Blumen. Seit 1929 offeriert die Kunstgärtnerei Doll exklusiven Blumenschmuck für jeden Anlass. Auf einer Verkaufsfläche von 3.500 Quadratmetern stehen exotische Gewächse einträchtig neben heimischen Pflanzen, herrliche Schnittblumen neben aufwendigen Blumenarrangements. Auch ausgesuchte Möbel, Töpfe und individuelle Dekoelemente mischen sich unter das hochwertige Angebot. Markenzeichen ist jedoch der „Doll-Strauß". Seit 20 Jahren verschönert die Kunstgärtnerei auch den Ball der Bälle, den Wiener Opernball, mit herrlichen Blumendekorationen.

Anyone who's ever entered the historic nursery in Nonntal valley knows: the name Doll stands for more than just flowers – it stands for flower art. At Doll's florists have been creating exclusive flower decorations for all occasions since 1929. On a sales area of 3,500 square meter exotic plants live peacefully next to local ones and stunning cut flowers next to intricate floral arrangements. Selected furniture items, pots, and individual decorative elements round off the high-quality range of goods on offer. The special trademark, however, is the "Doll-bouquet". For more than 20 years the flower artists at Doll have been in charge of decorating the ball of balls, Vienna's Opera Ball, with wonderful flower arrangements.

Öffnungszeiten:

Gärtnerei:
Mo – Sa
8 – 18.30 Uhr
So & Feiertag:
9 – 16 Uhr

Gegenüber dem Stammhaus lockt mit dem „Vis-à-Vis" ein kleines, individuelles Doll-Kaffeehaus.

Vis-à-Vis:
Mo – Sa:
10 – 18 Uhr

Opening hours:

Nursery:
Mon – Sat
8 am – 6.30 pm
Sun & public holidays
9 am – 4 pm

Just across the street from their original store a small, individual café called "Vis-á-Vis" beckons

Vis-á-Vis
Mon – Sat
10 am – 6 pm

KUNSTGÄRTNEREI DOLL
Nonntaler Hauptstrasse 79, 5020 Salzburg
Tel. +43 662 / 8218 290
office@doll-salzburg.at, www.doll-salzburg.at

VIS-À-VIS DOLL CAFÉ
Nonntaler Hauptstrasse 108, 5020 Salzburg
Tel. +43 662 / 8218 29-30

Luis Trenker

LUIS TRENKER

Italienischer Spirit mitten in Salzburg

Seit Februar 2019 gibt es die beliebte alpine Lifestyle-Marke Luis Trenker auch in der schönen Mozartstadt. Mit dem Shop in Salzburg kehrt Geschäftsführer Michi Klemera zurück zu seinen Wurzeln. Denn von 1897 bis 1928 gab es in der Linzergasse einen Schneidermeister und k&k Hoflieferant – Wenzel Klemera, seines Zeichens Urgroßvater von Michi Klemera. In der Judengasse im Herzen von Salzburg wird nun auf einer Fläche von über 170 Quadratmetern die komplette Lifestylewelt mit den Kollektionen Luis Trenker sowie der Outdoorkollektion Luis Trenker berg präsentiert. Eine breite Palette von schicken Accessoires runden eine Auswahl ab, die nicht nur die Herzen von Luis Trenker-Fans höherschlagen lässt.

As of February 2019 the popular lifestyle brand Luis Trenker has also found a home in the beautiful city of Mozart. With the new shop in Salzburg manager Michi Klemera returns to his roots. Because between 1897 and 1928 there was a master tailor and purveyor to the court in Salzburg's Linzergasse – and his name was Wenzel Klemera, great-grand-father of Michi Klemera. Now the new 170 square meters shop in Judengasse at the heart of Salzburg will present the entire lifestyle world with the Luis Trenker collections as well as the Luis Trenker berg outdoor collection. A wide range of accessories rounds off the large variety that will not just amaze Luis Trenker fans.

Öffnungszeiten:
Mo - Fr
9.30 - 18 Uhr
Sa
9.30 - 17 Uhr

Opening hours:
Mon - Fri
9.30 am - 6 pm
Sat
9.30 am - 5 pm

LUIS TRENKER SHOP SALZBURG
Judengasse 9, 5020 Salzburg
Tel. +43 662 / 8411 73
shop@luistrenker.com, www.luistrenker.com

© Foto: Luis Trenker

SCHEICHER

Designklassiker von Morgen

Im Einrichtungshaus Scheicher pflegt man seit 1923 die Achtsamkeit gegenüber Architektur und Design. Familie Scheicher ist seit Generationen mit europäischem Design eng verbunden und entwickelt Gesamtlösungen für ein qualitätsvolles, beständiges und nachhaltiges Wohnen und Arbeiten. Dabei gilt stets die Herausforderung, Einrichtungsobjekte anzubieten, die an Funktion und Design unübertrefflich sind und ein Leben lang Freude bereiten. Mit diesen hohen Ansprüchen entstehen weltweit exklusive private Wohnbereiche, Küchen, Büros, Shop-Konzepte, Banken bis hin zu Gastronomiebetrieben und Hotels. Das Einrichtungshaus Scheicher ist offizieller Fachhandelspartner von rund 250 internationalen Möbelherstellern und zertifizierter Store für maßgefertigte Hästens Premium-Betten.

Since 1923 the furniture store Einrichtungshaus Scheicher has always been about mindfully working with architecture and design. The Scheicher family has been closely connected to European design for generations and develops holistic solutions for high-quality, lasting, and sustainable living and working. Thereby the main challenge always is that of finding furnishings that are the best in terms of design and function and that will make clients happy all life long. Exclusive private living environments, kitchens, offices, shop concepts, banks, and even restaurants and hotels created across the globe all meet those high-quality standards. Einrichtungshaus Scheicher is an official trading partner of around 250 international furniture makers and a certified store for tailor-made Hästens premium beds.

Öffnungszeiten:
Mo - Fr
10 - 18.15 Uhr
Sa 10 - 14 Uhr

Opening hours:
Mon - Fri
10 am - 6.15 pm
Sat 10 am - 2 pm

EINRICHTUNGSHAUS SCHEICHER & HÄSTENS STORE SALZBURG
Neutorstrasse 18, 5020 Salzburg
Tel. +43 662 / 8453 13
office@scheicher.net, www.scheicher.net

STILLSEGLER

Handwerk oder Kunstwerk

Manche Dinge geben die Sorgfalt und Liebe, die während der Entstehung in sie einfließen, an ihre Betrachter und Benützer weiter. Die bunte Vielfalt der Stillsegler-Kollektion bietet Überraschendes aus längst verloren geglaubten Produktionsformen. Stillsegler unterstützt seit vielen Jahren langbewährte Manufakturen, die sich meist seit Generationen in Familienbesitz befinden. Diese Manufakturen sind Spezialisten auf ihrem Gebiet und machen die außergewöhnliche Sortimentsgestaltung von Stillsegler möglich. Offeriert werden auf höchstem handwerklichen Niveau hergestellte Produkte mit durchdachtem Design, die unter fairen Arbeitsbedingungen ökologisch nachhaltig produziert wurden.

Some things simply pass all the diligence and passion which were poured into them during production on to those looking at them and using them. The colourful variety of the Stillsegler collection contains surprising pieces that were made using long-forgotten methods of production. Stillsegler has been supporting long-established manufactories for many years, most of which have been family-owned for generations. These manufactories are specialitsts in their field and they are who make the unusual range of products offered at Stillsegler possible. It is made up of products made at the highest level of craftsmanship; with well thought out design, made under fair working conditions, and ecologically stustainable.

Öffnungszeiten:
Mo - Fr
10 - 13 Uhr &
13.30 - 18 Uhr
Sa 10 - 16 Uhr

Opening hours:
Mon - Fri
10 am - 1 pm &
1.30 pm - 6 pm
Sat 10 am - 4 pm

STILLSEGLER
Herbert-von-Karajan-Platz 3, 5020 Salzburg
Tel. +43 662 / 8404 58
salzburg@stillsegler.com, www.stillsegler.com

WIMMER SCHNEIDERT

Handgefertigte Lieblingsstücke mit Tradition

Eine handgemachte Lederhose, ein hochwertiges Dirndl, ein fescher Janker – Tracht ist modern wie nie. Kein Wunder: In den traditionsreichen Kleidungsstücken macht jeder eine gute Figur. Mit Tradition kennt sich auch Wimmer schneidert bestens aus – seit 1741 steht der Familienbetrieb für maßgefertigte Tracht und Trachtenmode. In der Schneiderei in Schleedorf, wo vor neun Generationen alles begann, werden Dirndl und Co. bis heute passgenau auf den Leib der Kunden geschneidert. Ob aus feinem Leinen, edler Seide oder robustem Hirschleder – hier entstehen echte Lieblingsstücke. Auch in der Stadt Salzburg kommt man in den Genuss der Wimmer-Tracht: Im Rochushof warten Lederhose, Dirndl, Trachtenröcke und mehr darauf, entdeckt zu werden. Und bei diesen schönen Stücken dauert das bestimmt nicht lange.

Handmade Lederhosen, a high-quality Dirndl dress, a chic jacket - traditional costume is hip. No wonder: the traditional garments look good on anyone. And "Wimmer schneidert" certainly know their way around tradition - the family-run business has been standing for tailor-made traditional costume and costume fashion since 1741. At the tailor shop in Schleedorf, where everything began nine generations ago, clients still get their Dirndl and co. fitted to perfection. Whether it's made from fine linen, precious silk or robust buckskin - this is where new favourite pieces are made. You'll also find Wimmer Tracht in the city of Salzburg: at Rochushof Lederhosen, Dirndl, traditional skirts and more are waiting to be discovered. And given the beauty of these items you won't want to wait long.

Öffnungszeiten:
Rochusgasse 6:
Mo – Fr
9.30 – 18 Uhr
Sa
9 – 12.30 Uhr

Öffnungszeiten:
Dorf 96:
Mo – Fr
8 – 12 Uhr und
13 – 18 Uhr
Sa
8 – 12 Uhr

Opening hours:
Rochusgasse 6:
Mon - Fri
9.30 am - 6 pm
Sat
9 am - 12.30 pm

Opening hours:
Dorf 96:
Mon – Fri
8 am – noon &
1 pm – 6 pm
Sat
8 am – noon

WIMMER SCHNEIDERT
Rochusgasse 6, 5020 Salzburg
Tel. +43 662 / 8240 80
lebensfreude@wimmertracht.at, www.wimmertracht.at

WIMMER SCHNEIDERT
Dorf 96, 5205 Schleedorf
Tel. +43 6216 / 6562

Restaurant & Hotel Guide

ANGUSTA

Fleischeslust und süsse Sünden

Irland beginnt am Wolfgangsee – zumindest in kulinarischer Hinsicht. Die Spezialität des Angusta in St. Gilgen ist echtes Angusrind von der grünen Atlantikinsel. Am Waldesrand gelegen begeistert das Restaurant seit mehr als zehn Jahren mit Fleischgerichten vom offenen Holzofengrill. Echt und authentisch ist die Devise des Eigentümerpaares Bettina und Aldo Zanatta – das trifft auch auf das Ambiente zu. Der Holztisch ist genauso ein Naturprodukt wie das Steak auf dem Teller, in den Sommermonaten zieht der Duft von Gräsern und Blumen über die Restaurantterrasse. Seit Kurzem kommen zur Fleischeslust süße Sünden hinzu: Ein kleines Café in St. Gilgen und Bad Ischl komplettiert das Genusserlebnis à la Angusta.

Who knew that Ireland borders on lake Wolfgangsee - at least as far as the culinary aspect is concerned. At Angusta in St. Gilgen the main specialty is real Angus beef from the green isle in the Atlantic. Located on the edge of the forest the restaurant has been treating its guests to meat dishes from its wood-fired grill for more than ten years. What's most important to the owners, Bettina and Aldo Zanatta, is that it's real and authentic - and that also goes for the ambiance. The wooden table is a natural product, just like the steak on the plate; and during the summer months the fragrance of grass and flowers pervades the restaurant's terrace. As of recently you can't just get meaty delicacies but sweet delights, too: in a small café in St. Gilgen and one in Bad Ischl. They perfectly round off the indulgent Angusta experience.

Öffnungszeiten:
Mi - So
17 - 24 Uhr

Opening hours:
Wed - Sun
5 pm - midnight

RESTAURANT ANGUSTA
Reitnerstrasse 48, 5340 Sankt Gilgen
Tel. +43 6227 / 21012
office@angusta.at, www.angusta.at

BIO-RESTAURANT HUMBOLDT

Das Lokal einer neuen Generation

Welche Zutaten braucht der Mensch, um glücklich zu sein? Geht es nach dem Bio-Restaurant Humboldt in der Salzburger Altstadt, dann nicht viele. Wohltuend schmackhaftes Essen, eine erholsame Atmosphäre und ein Feierabendgetränk in netter Gesellschaft – so einfach ist die Humboldt-Formel für ein zufriedenes, entschleunigtes Leben. In der neuen Humboldt-Stubn besinnen sich Jung und Alt der Urform des Genießens; mit biodynamischen Gerichten, dem achtsamen Umgang miteinander, coolen Klängen am Wochenende und feinen Tropfen zum Wecken der guten Geister. Das alles bietet das Bio-Restaurant Humboldt, und noch ein bisschen mehr: eine entspannte Auszeit im Lokal einer neuen Generation.

What ingredients does it need to make someone happy? If you listen to the people of organic restaurant Humboldt – not all that many. Beneficial, tasty food in a relaxing atmosphere and an after-work drink in good company; that's the Humboldt-formula for a happy, relaxed life. At the new Humboldt-Stubn parlour young and old can find their way back to the original forms of indulgence; with biodynamic dishes, mindful interactions with one another, cool sounds on the weekends, and a fine vintage to awaken the spirit. All this can be found at Bio-Restaurant Humboldt, and even a little more: a relaxed time-out in the restaurant of a new generation.

Öffnungszeiten:
So - Do
11.30 - 24 Uhr
Fr & Sa
11.30 - 2 Uhr

Warme Küche
bis 22 Uhr

Während der Festspielzeit:
Warme Küche
bis 23 Uhr

Opening hours:
Sun - Thu
11.30 am - midnight
Fri & Sat
11.30 am - 2 am

Warm food served until 10 pm

During Festspielzeit: warm food served until 11 pm

BIO-RESTAURANT HUMBOLDT
Gstättengasse 4, 5020 Salzburg
Tel. +43 662 / 8431 71
info@humboldtstubn.at, www.humboldtstubn.at

BLAUE GANS

Urban Gourmet-Hideway im Herzen von Salzburg

Zwischen Getreidegasse und Karajan-Platz versteckt sich ein Geheimtipp für Genießer. Die Blaue Gans ist Salzburgs ältestes Gasthaus und gleichzeitig das erste und einzige Arthotel der Stadt. Design, Individualität und rund 120 Kunstwerke zeichnen das Haus aus, seit es Eigentümer Andreas Gfrerer behutsam renoviert hat. Als Refugium für Genießer speist man in der Blauen Gans vorzüglich – im historischen Gewölbe wie in der modernen Brasserie-Bar, die lässigen Großstadtflair versprüht. Hier treffen sich Leute mit entspannter Lebensanschauung, um gute Drinks und die lockere Atmosphäre zu genießen – und das Essen! Ganztags gibt´s Snacks und köstliches Fingerfood, auch mehrgängige Menüs für den großen Hunger. Perfekt für eine Shopping-Pause! Und im Schanigarten vor der spektakulären Mönchsbergwand lässt es sich ebenfalls genüsslich die Zeit vergessen.

Tucked away between Getreidegasse and Karajan-Platz epicures will find a true insider tip here. Blaue Gans is Salzburg's oldest inn and at the same time it also is the city's first and only arthotel. Design, individuality, and around 120 works of art have been characterising the place since its careful renovation at the hands of owner Andreas Gfrerer. As a refuge for gourmets the Blaue Gans offers excellent cuisine – served under the historic vaulted ceiling of the restaurant or at the modern brasserie-bar with its cool urban flair. A meeting place for all those with a relaxed attitude towards life, who come here for good drinks and the laid-back atmosphere – and the food! Snacks and delicious finger food are served all day, so are multiple-course menus for anyone who's really hungry. Perfect for a time-out from shopping! And the outdoor area at the foot of the spectacular rock face of Mönchsberg is a wonderful spot and perfect to indulge and lose track of time.

Öffnungszeiten:
Mo - Sa
12 - 24 Uhr

Warme Küche
bis 22 Uhr

Bei Schönwetter
Gastgarten
geöffnet

Opening hours:
Mon - Sat
noon - midnight

Warm food served
until 10 pm

Open-air restaurant
open in good
weather

BLAUE GANS
Getreidegasse 41 – 43, 5020 Salzburg
Tel. +43 662 / 8424 91
office@blauegans.at, www.blauegans.at

DAS EDELWEISS

Restaurant & Hotel Guide

Ein Resort blüht auf

Aktiv- und Entspannungsurlaub in einem, all das und noch mehr bietet DAS EDELWEISS ab Juli 2019 seinen Gästen. Eingebettet in die malerische Berglandschaft des Großarltals, hat sich das ehemalige Hotel Edelweiss der Gastgeberfamilie Hettegger zu einem Luxusresort mit 148 Zimmern und Suiten gewandelt. Durch die Lage in der wunderschönen Berg- und Almenwelt Salzburg ist das Hotel Ausgangspunkt für zahlreiche Aktivprogramme und Ihre Premium-Auszeit – ob man gemeinsam mit Partner, Freunden oder Familie die Natur erforschen, in den Bergen Neues erleben oder einfach entspannen möchte. Besonderes Highlight: Der Wellnessbereich nur für Erwachsene und jener für Familien mit großem Indoor-Rutschenpark und einem abgetrennten Saunabereich.

Active and relaxing holidays all in one – this and even more promises DAS EDELWEISS. Opening in July 2019 and nestled in the picture-postcard mountain landscape of the Grossarl Valley, host family Hettegger transformed the former Hotel Edelweiss into a luxury resort with 148 rooms and suites. The beautiful world of Salzburg's mountains and alpine pastures makes the hotel an ideal starting place for numerous activities and an excellent retreat for well-deserved breaks – experience nothing but nature, explore the mountains, or simply sit back and relax with your partner, friends or family. Special highlight: the spa for adults as well as the family area with indoor slide park and a separate sauna section.

Tagesgäste sind im Day Spa herzlich willkommen.

Day guests are more than welcome at the Day Spa.

DAS EDELWEISS SALZBURG MOUNTAIN RESORT
Unterbergstrasse 65, 5611 Grossarl
Tel. +43 6414 / 3000
info@edelweiss-grossarl.com, www.edelweiss-grossarl.com

DER SEEHOF

Hotel und Restaurant in den Salzburger Alpen

Restaurant & Hotel Guide

Liebevoll Verzauberungsanstalt genannt, macht es beim Betreten des Hotels Der Seehof eher den Anschein, man wäre in einem großen Wohnzimmer gelandet. An den Wänden hängt zeitgenössische Kunst, in den Regalen steht eine ausgewählte Bibliothek mit allen Suhrkamp-Erstausgaben. Die Gastgeber Susi und Sepp Schellhorn schufen individuelle Zimmer für jeden Geschmack, die am Kraftplatz Goldegg zu einer Wohlfühloase werden. Ein Spaziergang um den Moorsee wird wärmstens empfohlen! Im Zwei-Hauben-Restaurant HECHT! r120 mit offener Küche überzeugt das herzliche Seehof-Team anspruchsvolle Gaumen mit nachhaltigen Produkten, die hauptsächlich aus einem Radius von bis zu 120 Kilometer stammen. Besonderes Highlight: Der Chef's Table, der für alle Gäste zugänglich ist.

Hotel Seehof was once nicknamed an "enchantment institute" and upon entering one can't help but feel as if it's one big living room. The walls are decorated with contemporary art, the shelves filled with selected books and all of Suhrkamp publishers' first editions. The hosts Sepp and Susi Schellhorn have created individual rooms for every taste thus turning the hotel in the place of power that is Goldegg into an oasis of wellbeing. A walk around Moorsee lake is warmly recommended!
A walk around Moorsee lake is warmly recommended! The 2-star restaurant HECHT! r120 with its Chef's Table that's accessible to all guests only uses sustainable products that are made no more than 120 kilometres away. A special highlight: the wonderful lake view terrace!

Öffnungszeiten:
HECHT! r120

Genussfrühstück:
Mo - So
8 - 11 Uhr, 28 €
Mittag:
12 - 14 Uhr
Fr / Sa / So
12 - 17 Uhr
Abend:
18.30 - 21 Uhr

Opening hours:
HECHT! r120

Indulgent breakfast:
Mon - Sun
8 am - 11 am, 28 €
Lunch:
noon - 2 pm
Fri / Sat / Sun
noon - 5 pm
Dinner:
6.30 pm - 9 pm

A LA CARTE **80**

falstaff **91**

HOTEL DER SEEHOF
Hofmark 8, 5622 Goldegg am See
Tel. +43 6415 / 81370
office@derseehof.at, www.derseehof.at

NEUSIEDLERSEE
NEUSIEDLERSEE - HÜGELLAND
CARNUNTUM
THERMENREGION
WIEN

DÖLLERER

Enoteca & Weinhandelshaus

Restaurant & Hotel Guide

In Döllerers Enoteca & Weinhandelshaus vor den Toren Gollings, in Kuchl, schlagen die Herzen von Genussmenschen höher. Bei einem Sortiment von mehr als 400.000 Flaschen aus über 230 Weingütern sowie Schaumwein- und Spirituosenerzeugern aus aller Welt finden Liebhaber von flüssigen kulinarischen Spezialitäten in jeder Preisklasse das Passende. Besonders originell ist die rundum verlaufende „Weinbibliothek", in der die flüssigen Schätze perfekt präsentiert werden. Offen, modern und zugleich unverkennbar italienisch ist die Enoteca außerdem ein Hotspot in Sachen Weinverkostungen, Feiern und Seminaren. Döllerers Genusspackerl, Alimentari, Accessoires und Bücher runden das vielfältige Sortiment ab und laden zum Verkosten, Schmökern und Kaufen ein.

Döllerer's Enoteca & Weinhandelshaus (= wine trading house) just outside Golling in Kuchl is every epicure's dream. With more than 400,000 bottles from more than 230 wineries, sparkling wine and spirit producers from all over the world, lovers of bottled culinary delights are sure to find the perfect vintage in every price class. What's particularly interesting is the circular "Wine Library" where the liquid treasures are perfectly presented. Open, modern, yet still very Italian – that makes the Enoteca ideal for wine tastings, celebrations, and workshops. Döllerer's Genusspackerl (= indulgence packages), alimentari, accessories, and books round off the varied product range and beckon you to taste, browse, and buy.

Öffnungszeiten:
Mo - Mi
9.30 - 18.30 Uhr
Do & Fr
9.30 - 23 Uhr
Sa 9.30 - 12.30 Uhr
So geschlossen

Opening hours:
Mon - Wed
9.30 am - 6.30 pm
Thu & Fri
9.30 am - 11 pm
Sat 9.30 am - 12.30 pm
Sun closing day

DÖLLERER ENOTECA & WEINHANDELSHAUS
Kellau 160, 5431 Kuchl
Tel. +43 6244 / 20567
weinhandel@doellerer.at, www.weinhandelshaus.at

DÖLLERER

Genießerrestaurant

Restaurant & Hotel Guide

In Döllerers Genießerrestaurant ist der Name Programm, denn mit seiner „Cuisine Alpine" entführt Andreas Döllerer die Feinschmecker auf eine kulinarische Genusswanderung durch die Salzburger Alpen. Tradition und Heimatverbundenheit sowie deren moderne Interpretation spiegeln sich in seinen Gerichten ebenso wider wie seine Wertschätzung für regionale Produkte. Die alpinen Menüs „Göllüberquerung" und „Oberjoch" werden je nach Wunsch von herrlichen Weinen aus einer der besten Weinkarten Österreichs perfekt ergänzt. Andreas Döllerers innovative Küchenlinie bescherte Döllerers Genießerrestaurant erst kürzlich 99 von 100 Punkten im Falstaff Restaurantguide 2019. Von A la Carte wurde es ebenfalls mit 99 Punkten zum besten Restaurant Österreichs gekürt.

At Döllerers Genießerrestaurant (= connoisseurs' restaurant) the name really says it all: with his "Cuisine Alpine" Andreas Döllerer takes epicures on a culinary indulgence tour through Salzburg's Alps. Tradition and a strong regional focus as well as modern interpretations thereof are reflected in his dishes - just like his appreciation of regional products. The alpine menus "Göllüberquerung" and "Oberjoch" can be complemented with delicious vintages from the wine list - which is one of the best in Austria. Andreas Döllerer's innovative cooking only recently won Döllerers Genießerrestaurant 99 out of 100 points in the Falstaff restaurant guide 2019. The A la Carte restaurant guide also awarded it 99 points and declared it Austria's best restaurant.

Öffnungszeiten:
Di - Fr
18 - 21.30 Uhr
Sa 12 - 21.30 Uhr
So geschlossen

Opening hours:
Tue - Fri
6 pm - 9.30 pm
Sat noon - 9.30 pm
Sun closing day

DÖLLERERS GENIESSERRESTAURANT
Markt 56, 5440 Golling
Tel. +43 6244 / 4220-0
office@doellerer.at, www.doellerer.at

FORSTHOFALM

Natur ist Freiheit im Holzhotel

Restaurant & Hotel Guide

Nichts müssen, aber alles ausprobieren dürfen, was Hotel und Umgebung zu bieten haben – dafür steht das Motto „Natur ist Freiheit", das sich Hotelier Markus Widauer und sein Team auf die Fahnen geschrieben haben. Ob Trampolin-Workout auf der Alm, Yogakurse auf der Dachterrasse, Touren mit dem E-Fatbike oder ein Bad im beheizten Rooftop-Pool des Sky Spa mit 360 Grad Schönheit im Blick – das Hotel auf 1.050 Metern Höhe bietet unzählige Möglichkeiten. Aus der „Forsthofalm Regenbogenküche" des Restaurants Kukka kommen Gerichte aus vorwiegend regionalen Biozutaten, die die Farben des Regenbogens abbilden. Durch das ganze Haus zieht der beruhigende Duft nach Holz, im SPAnorama duftet es nach aromatischen Kräutern – und das ganzheitliche Almwellness-Erlebnis in den Bergen ist perfekt.

Not having to do anything but being allowed to try everything the hotel and its surroundings have to offer – that's what the motto "Nature is Freedom" that hotel owner Markus Widauer and his team have subscribed to is all about. Whether it's a trampoline workout on the alp, yoga courses on the roof terrace, e-fatbike tours, or a dip in the heated rooftop pool of the Sky Spa with its stunning 360 degree view of the surrounding beauty – the hotel at 1,050 metres above sea level offers so many possibilities. The "Forsthofalm rainbow kitchen" of Kukka restaurant delivers dishes that are made mostly from organic ingredients and that depict all the colours of the rainbow. The entire house is infused with the lovely fragrance of wood, the SPAnorama smells like aromatic herbs – and the holistic alpine wellness experience in the mountains is just perfect.

Besondere Arrangements finden Sie unter www.forsthofalm.com

Special arrangements and packages can be found on www.forsthofalm.com

HOLZHOTEL FORSTHOFALM
Hütten 37, 5771 Leogang
Tel. +43 6583 / 8545
info@forsthofalm.com, www.forsthofalm.com

GENUSSDORF GMACHL

Restaurant & Hotel Guide

Ein Dorf voller hausgemachter Genüsse

Anno 1787 begann alles ganz bodenständig. Fuhrleute suchten mit ihren Rössern eine Herberge und etwas Nahrung für Tier und Mensch. Damals trafen sich in Bergheim bereits Reisende, erholten sich vom anstrengenden Alltag – labten Körper, Geist und Seele, tankten Energie. Vielleicht spürt man deshalb im dörflich-urbanen Genussdorf Gmachl heute noch die Prinzipien eines Dorflebens: am Boden bleiben, die Natur respektieren, die Menschen schätzen und das Echte bewahren. Natürliche Materialien, ehrliche Rohstoffe, aufrichtige Beziehungen. Dazu schöne Wohnzimmer, gemütliche Stuben, ein Vitarium Spa voller Erfrischungen, einen Hauben-Gasthof, den Dorfladen, das FRANZ Dorfwirtshaus und den hauseigenen Brauer und Metzger.

Back in 1787 everything was still very much down to earth. Carters with their horses were looking for shelter and sustenance for both, animal and man. Back then travellers already met up in Bergheim where they were able to recover from the toils of their everyday lives - they refreshed their body, mind, and soul and recharged their batteries. Maybe that's why the indulgent village of Gmachl with its rural yet urban flair still seems to live by the principles of bucolic life: stay down to earth, respect nature, value people, and preserve what's authentic. Natural materials, genuine raw products, honest relationships. Beautiful living spaces, comfortable rooms, a Vitarium Spa full of refreshments, an haute cuisine inn, a village grocer, FRANZ village inn, and a brewer and butcher in the same house.

13 GAULT&MILLAU

GENUSSDORF GMACHL
HOTEL|SPA|RESTAURANT
Dorfstrasse 35, 5101 Bergheim
Tel. +43 662 / 4521 240
info@gmachl.at, www.gmachl.at

GOLDGASSE

Hotel & Gasthof

Restaurant & Hotel Guide

Abseits des Trubels, aber mitten in der historischen Salzburger Altstadt, liegt das Hotel Goldgasse. Ein Hotel, das nicht nur durch seine Einzigartigkeit bezaubert, sondern in seinen 16 individuellen Zimmern mit Luxus und viel Liebe zum Detail überzeugt. Spuren der rund 700-jährigen Vergangenheit des Hauses wurden subtil in das neue Konzept eingebaut. Highlight: die großformatigen Fotografien der Festspiele in jedem Zimmer. Wohlfühlen kann so einfach sein!
Der gleichnamige Gasthof ist ein Stern am kulinarischen Himmel der Stadt. Herausragende Haubenküche trifft hier auf besondere Gastfreundschaft. Verwöhnt werden Gäste mit österreichischen Klassikern, wie dem stadtbekannten Backhendl im Kupfertopf und den Salzburger Nockerln.

Away from the hustle and bustle but still at the centre of Salzburg's historic old town. A hotel that does not just enchant with its uniqueness but also impresses with 16 individual and luxurious rooms that were furbished with a lot of passion for detail. The traces of the house's 700-year-old history were incorporated into the new concept in a subtle fashion. Highlight: the large-format photographs from Salzburg Festival in every room. Feeling comfy can be so easy! The eponymous inn is a highlight of the city's culinary landscape. Excellent award-winning cuisine meets wonderful hospitality. Guests are treated to Austrian classics, such as the fried chicken in a copper pot that is known all over town and the famous Salzburger Nockerl.

Öffnungszeiten:
Täglich 7 - 23 Uhr

Warme Küche
bis 22 Uhr

Opening hours:
Daily 7 am - 11 pm

Warm food served
until 10 pm

HOTEL GOLDGASSE
Goldgasse 10, 5020 Salzburg
Tel. +43 662 / 8456 22
info@hotelgoldgasse.at
www.hotelgoldgasse.at

GASTHOF GOLDGASSE
Goldgasse 10, 5020 Salzburg
Tel. +43 662 / 8482 00
info@gasthofgoldgasse.at
www.gasthofgoldgasse.at

HAUS HIRT

Ein Hideway jenseits der Zeit

Restaurant & Hotel Guide

Fast wähnt man sich in einem Märchen, wenn man das wunderschöne Haus Hirt betritt. Liebevoll und detailverliebt renoviert, präsentiert sich das ehemalige Landhaus aus den 1920er-Jahren bis heute entrückt der Zeit und doch mit modernem Esprit. Es ist eine intime Wohlfühloase, in die Evelyn und Ike ihre Gäste einladen. Kurzum: Das Haus Hirt in Bad Gastein ist ein Hideaway, das diesen Begriff tatsächlich verdient. Weit weg von allem, kann man sich hier der Muße hingeben, beim Yoga Geist und Körper in Einklang bringen, beim Wandern die Gasteiner Bergwelt erobern, im Wellnessbereich das Panorama genießen und beim abendlichen Aperitif pure, alpine Schönheit vor Augen haben. Auch Familien mit Kindern sind ausdrücklich erwünscht – das Hotel Hirt ist ein kinderfreundliches Designhotel.

Upon entering stunningly beautiful Haus Hirt it almost feels like you're in a fairy tale. Renovated with passion and an eye for detail the former country estate from the 1920s still presents itself as lost in time yet with modern esprit. It's an intimate oasis of wellbeing where guests are welcomed by the hosts Evelyn and Ike. In short: Haus Hirt in Bad Gastein is a hideaway that truly deserves the name. Far away from everything you can just indulge and let yourself be inspired, reunite body and soul during yoga, conquer Gastein's mountains during a hike, enjoy the view in the wellness area and take in the stunning alpine beauty during aperitif in the evening. Families with children are warmly welcome – Hotel Hirt is a child-friendly design hotel.

Aveda Spa Treatments (bitte um Reservierung) & Yoga 2 x täglich inkludiert

Sommersaison:
29. Mai - 03. Nov 2019
Wintersaison:
05. Dez - 19. Apr 2020

Mitgliedschaften:
White Line Hotels - Urlaubsarchitektur

Auszeichnungen:
Gault&Millau „Hotel des Jahres 2019"

Aveda Spa Treatments (please book in advance) & yoga 2 times a day included

Summer Season:
29 May - 03 Nov 2019
Winter Season:
05 Dec - 19 Apr 2020

Memberships:
White Line Hotels - Urlaubsarchitektur

Awards: Gault&Millau "Hotel of the Year 2019"

HAUS HIRT HOTEL & SPA
Kaiserhofstrasse 14, 5640 Bad Gastein
Tel. +43 6434 / 27970
booking@haus-hirt.com www.haus-hirt.com

HOTEL SCHLOSS LEOPOLDSKRON

Restaurant & Hotel Guide

Feiern, Tagen & Übernachten mit historischem Flair in Salzburg

Das 1736 erbaute, von einem sieben Hektar großen Park umgebene Schloss liegt an einem kleinen, idyllischen Weiher mit herrlicher Aussicht auf die Berge und die Festung Hohensalzburg.
Mit 55 Zimmern im Meierhof, zwölf Suiten im Schloss und zwei Townhäusern ist das historische Schloss Leopoldskron ein diskreter Rückzugsort nur wenige Minuten von der Salzburger Altstadt entfernt.
Es ist auch der ideale Veranstaltungsort für Seminare, Workshops, Konferenzen und Events.

Built in 1736, and surrounded by seven acres of manicured grounds, Schloss Leopoldskron is nestled by a small, idyllic lake, and features majestic views of the mountains and the Hohensalzburg Fortress.
With 55 rooms in the Meierhof, twelve suites in the historic palace, and two townhouses, Schloss Leopoldskron is an exclusive and discreet hideaway just minutes from the Old Town of Salzburg.
It is also the ideal venue for seminars, workshops, conferences, weddings, and events.

Tipp:
Shakespeare im Park: Love Songs Premiere ab 22. Mai 2019

Tag der offenen Tür am 17. Nov 2019 unter dem Motto „The Sound of Christmas"

Silvester-Galadinner Reservierungen unter events@schloss-leopoldskron.com

Besondere Übernachtunsgsangebote finden Sie unter www.schloss-leopoldskron.com

For special package deals, see www.schloss-leopoldskron.com

HOTEL SCHLOSS LEOPOLDSKRON
Leopoldskronstrasse 56 – 58, 5020 Salzburg
Tel. +43 662 / 8398 30
reception@schloss-leopoldskron.com, www.schloss-leopoldskron.com

DON'T PANIC
FOR EVERYONE OVER 21

HOTEL SEPP

Alpine Boutique Hotel für Gäste ab 21

Restaurant & Hotel Guide

Außergewöhnlich. Einzigartig. Bemerkenswert. Eben "exSEPP-tional". Das ist der Anspruch vom SEPP. Unter dem Motto „gemeinsam mittendrin" zelebrieren Gäste hier das Leben in stylisch-lässigem Ambiente und unkonventioneller Wohfühl-Atmosphäre. Adults-only-Konzept, Design-Raffinessen, Lieblingsplätze und extravagante Details geben dem Hotel eine einzigartige Note für das Lebensgefühl der besonderen Art. Sport, Micro-Events und Motto-Weekends bringen die Menschen zusammen. Gleichzeitig gibt es genug Raum im Haus für individuelle Rückzugsmomente. Das stylische Lifestylehotel für Gäste ab 21 Jahren versteht sich als außergewöhnlicher Ort für schöne Begegnungen, besondere Lebensqualität, echte Glücksgefühle und viele Genuss- und Wohlfühlmomente.

Extraordinary. Unique. Remarkable. Simply "exSepp-tional". That's SEPP's goal. Under the motto "together right in the middle" guests celebrate life in a stylish and cool setting with an unconventional feel-good atmosphere. Adults-only concept, sophisticated design, favourite spots, and extravagant design make this hotel so particular, infusing it with a special kind of joie de vivre. Sports, micro events, and motto weekends bring people together. At the same time the house offers plenty of room for individual moments of quiet. The stylish lifestyle hotel for guests aged 21 and above sees itself as an extraordinary spot for beautiful encounters, special quality of life, real happiness, and many moments of indulgence and wellbeing.

Adults-only-Konzept

Brunch bis 13 Uhr im Preis inkludiert

40 Zimmer mit verschiedenen Highlights: Plattenspieler, freistehende Badewanne, Heimkino, Panoramafenster

Dachboden mit Open Space & Roof Top Lounge

Airstream-Sauna & Infinity Pool

"Adults-only" concept

Brunch until 1 pm included in the price

40 rooms with various highlights: record player, freestanding tub, home cinema, panoramic window

Attic with open space & rooftop lounge

Airstream sauna & infinity pool

HOTEL SEPP
Urchen 8, 5761 Maria Alm
Tel. +43 6584 / 7738
info@ederhotels.com, www.edersepp.com

KOLLER + KOLLER TAGESBAR

Restaurant & Hotel Guide

Da trifft sich´s gut

Schon alleine durch seine prominente Lage ist das K+K am Waagplatz ein wichtiger Bestandteil des kulturellen und gesellschaftlichen Lebens der Stadt Salzburg. Mit der neuen Tagesbar im Erdgeschoss bietet das Traditionshaus neben seinen gemütlichen Stuben nun eine weitere Gelegenheit für geselliges Beisammensein. Diese besticht optisch insbesondere durch eine faszinierende Architektur. Patinierte Messingmosaikplatten zieren die gesamte Gewölbedecke und sind der Eyecatcher schlechthin! Natürlich ist die Tagesbar auch kulinarisch ein Erlebnis. Österreichische Klassiker mit raffinierter Zubereitung passen hervorragend zu den Wein- und Bierspezialitäten oder Barklassikern wie Negroni und Co.

Its prominent location on Waagplatz alone makes K+K an important element of the city of Salzburg's cultural and social fabric. With its new daytime bar on the ground floor the traditional house now offers yet another perfect spot for friendly get-togethers – aside from its cosy parlours. The bar impresses with its fascinating architecture. Patinised brass mosaic plates decorate the entire vaulted ceiling – really, quite the eye catcher! And, of course, the day bar also offers culinary delights. Austrian classics are prepared with finesse and they go perfectly with excellent wines and beers as well as classics from the bar, such as Negroni and Co.

Öffnungszeiten:
Mo, Do, Fr & Sa
11 – 23 Uhr
So 11 – 17 Uhr
Di & Mi: Ruhetag

Juli, August & September:
Kein Ruhetag!

Opening hours:
Mon, Thu, Fri & Sat
11 am – 11 pm
Sun 11 - 5 pm
Tue & Wed: closing days

July, August & September:
no closing days!

KOLLER + KOLLER TAGESBAR
Waagplatz 2, 5020 Salzburg
Tel. +43 662 / 8421 56
talk@kollerkoller.com, www.kollerkoller.com

M32

Alles Gute kommt von oben

Restaurant & Hotel Guide

Von oben sieht die Welt ganz anders aus. Davon kann man sich im Restaurant M32 im Museum der Moderne am Mönchsberg selbst überzeugen. Den imposanten Ausblick auf die Stadt genießt man in netter Gesellschaft von einer der schönsten Terrassen Salzburgs. Ein Blick in die Speisekarte eröffnet Kulinarik auf Haubenniveau, die jedoch nie die Bodenhaftung verliert: Wiener Schnitzel vom Kalb trifft auf gegrillten Pulpo und klassische Marillenpalatschinken. Auch für den perfekten Start in den Tag bietet das M32 zahlreiche Frühstücksvariationen, die in höchsten Höhen den Morgen versüßen. Und wer noch eine Eventlocation für Hochzeiten, Firmenfeiern und Familienessen sucht, der findet im M32 ebenfalls inspirierende Räumlichkeiten für jeden Anlass.

Seen from above the world looks so different. And at restaurant M32 in Salzburg's museum of modern art (Museum der Moderne) guests can see for themselves. The impressive view of the city is best enjoyed in pleasant company and on one of Salzburg's most beautiful terraces. A glance at the menu reveals haute cuisine that is never aloof: Viennese veal schnitzel meets grilled pulpo and classic apricot crepes. And the numerous breakfast varieties available at M32 guarantee a perfect start to the day with the highest indulgence. And all those looking for an event location for weddings, corporate events, and family meals will also find inspiring spaces for every occasion at M32.

Öffnungszeiten:
Di - So
9 - 1 Uhr

Opening hours:
Tue - Sun
9 am - 1 am

14
GAULT&MILLAU

RESTAURANT M32
im Museum der Moderne
Mönchsberg 32, 5020 Salzburg
Tel. +43 662 / 8410 00
info@m32.at, www.m32.at

MAGAZIN:

wine. food. people. music.

Restaurant & Hotel Guide

Im Salzburger magazin: betreibt man nach Jahren der Sterneküche ein offenes Bistro. An einem Ort, der fast alles ist, außer gewöhnlich. An sich schon sehenswert: die moderne Architektur, welche sich sanft an den Felsen der Mönchsbergwand schmiegt. Gäste erwartet ein Potpourri der Kulinarik mit herrlichen Gaumenfreuden zum Hier-Genießen oder Mit-nach-Hause-Nehmen sowie heimelige Lieblingsecken. Mit allerlei Erlesenem aus dem hauseigenen Wein- und Spezialitätenhandel, das bestaunt und verkostet werden will, ergibt sich so ein völlig neues kulinarisches Konzept, das durch seine erfrischende Lockerheit besticht. Das Publikum ist jung, der Service unkompliziert, die Stimmung leger. Ein Ort mit vielen Facetten – und ganz ohne Hemmschwellen.

After years of haute cuisine Salzburg's magazin: now runs an open bistro. A place that is almost anything except ordinary. Quite the eye-catcher: modern architecture gently hugs the rock of the Mönchsberg's wall. Guests can expect a mixture of excellent culinary delights to eat in or take home and plenty of cosy favourite corners. The house's wine and delicatessen shop has quite a lot to admire and try - and it is part of a completely new culinary concept that impresses with its casual charm. The guests are young, the service is low-key, and the atmosphere relaxed. A place with many facets and without inhibitions.

Öffnungszeiten:
Di – Sa
10 – 24 Uhr

Im August und Dezember auch montags geöffnet

Opening hours:
Tue – Sat
10 am – midnight

Open on Mondays in August and December

MAGAZIN:
Claudia und Raimund Katterbauer
Augustinergasse 13, 5020 Salzburg
Tel. +43 662 / 8415 84
office@magazin.co.at, www.magazin.co.at

Voi
LÄSSIG!

MAMA THRESL

Tradition und Moderne perfekt kombiniert

„urban soul meets the alps" lautet das Motto des mama thresl, das den Gästen mit seinem lässigen Konzept ein Stück alpin-sportliches Zuhause bietet. Den Inhabern Renate und Huwi Oberlader gelingt eine perfekte Symbiose aus Tradition und Moderne, Natürlichkeit und hochwertigem Design. Ein Klettersteig an der Außenfassade und eine Indoor-Kletterwand sind nur zwei Beispiele für die sportliche Ausrichtung. Bergfreunde wie Mountainbiker und Wanderer starten direkt vom mama thresl in die Natur, profitieren von einer perfekten Infrastruktur und freuen sich über 400 Kilometer Wegenetz. In den angrenzenden Leoganger Steinbergen laden neun Yoga-Plattformen zum Relaxen in der Natur ein; allein oder bei Kursen mit Renate Oberlader – die Chefin ist ausgebildete Yogalehrerin.

"urban soul meets the Alps" is the motto of mama thresl, which treats its guests to the casual concept of a mountain sports home. The owners, Renate and Huwi Oberlader, created the perfect symbiosis between tradition and modernity, authenticity and premium design. A via ferrata along the outside façade and an indoor climbing wall are just two examples of mama thresl's sports focus. Alpine aficionados, mountain bikers and hikers can head straight off into nature and benefit not only from the ideal infrastructure but also from more than 400 kilometres of trails. The surrounding Leogang Mountains offer a welcome retreat with nine yoga platforms in the midst of nature – either alone or with Renate Oberlader, as the boss is also a trained yoga instructor.

MAMA THRESL
Sonnberg 252, 5771 Leogang
Tel. +43 6583 / 20800
info@mama-thresl.com, www.mama-thresl.com

HENDL FISCHEREI
Tel. +43 6583 / 20800-800

SCHLOSS FUSCHL RESORT & SPA

Restaurant & Hotel Guide

Wo man zu träumen beginnt ...

Am Ufer des türkisblauen Fuschlsees gelegen und von Bergen und Wäldern umgeben, ist Schloss Fuschl der perfekte Ort zum Träumen. Das herrliche Ambiente des aus Sissi-Filmen bekannten Schlosses lädt dazu ein, die Seele baumeln zu lassen. Hier ist sie, die stille Idylle jenseits der Zeit, nach der sich nicht nur vielbeschäftigte Großstädter sehnen. Sie wirkt umso tiefer, weil sie mit modernem Luxus kombiniert ist: fangfrische Fische aus der hauseigenen Fischerei, eine Weinkarte mit 6.000 Positionen, exklusive Haupthauszimmer und -Suiten sowie sechs charmante Privatvillen mit eigenem Seegrundstück. Ein kleines, aber feines Spa und ein Heli-Port perfektionieren das Bild. Der Balanceakt zwischen gestern, heute und morgen gelingt perfekt, was nicht nur Royals, Staatsmänner und Filmstars schätzen.

Situated on the shore of turquoise-coloured Fuschlsee lake and surrounded by mountains and forests, Schloss Fuschl castle really is the perfect place to dream. The wonderful ambiance of the castle that is well-known from the Sissi-movies simply beckons you to step in and relax. This is it, the spot where quiet, idyllic surroundings defeat time and give the busy city dweller exactly what they were yearning for. And the effect is all the more profound when combined with modern luxury: fresh fish from the house's own fishery, a wine list with 6,000 positions, exclusive rooms and suites in the main building as well as six charming private villas on the lakeshore. A small but exquisite spa and a heliport to round it all off.

Jahresbetrieb

Öffnungszeiten:
Restaurant:
19 - 21.30 Uhr
Bar:
11.00 - 23.00 Uhr

Reservierungen unter
+43 6229 / 22530
oder info@schloss-fuschl.com

Open year round

Opening hours:
Restaurant:
7 pm - 9.30 pm
Bar:
11 am - 11 pm

For reservations, call
+43 6229 / 22530
or e-mail
info@schlossfuschl.com

SCHLOSS FUSCHL RESORT & SPA
Schloss-Strasse 19, 5322 Hof bei Salzburg
Tel. +43 6229 / 2253
info@schlossfuschl.com, www.schlossfuschlsalzburg.com

SENNS. RESTAURANT

Spitzenküche im Gusswerk

„Wer nie die ausgetrampelten Pfade verlässt, kommt nur dort an, wo andere schon waren“, lautet die Devise von SENNS. Restaurant. In einer ehemaligen Glockengießerei, wo früher in Brennöfen Metall geschmolzen und gegossen wurde, ist nun das sternen- und haubengekrönte Restaurant beheimatet. Im industriellen Charme kommen Gästen in den Genuss der Spitzenküche des Chefkochs Andreas Senn, der erstklassige Speisen aus Österreich und der ganzen Welt serviert. Das SENNS.Restaurant ist kulinarischer Melting Pot, der Feinschmecker-Gaumen abends mit einem Vier- bis Acht-Gänge-Menü überrascht. Mittags steht ein genussvolles Drei-und Vier-Gang-Menü zur Wahl.

The motto at SENNS.Restaurant: "If you never chose to leave the trodden path you'll only every get where everyone else has been before." Located in a former bell foundry, a place where furnaces smoked and metal was melted, the premises now host an award-winning restaurant. Surrounded by the location's industrial charm the guests get to indulge in the award-winning haute cuisine made by chef Andreas Senn who serves excellent dishes from Austria and all over the world. SENNS.Restaurant is a culinary melting pot where epicures are surprised with four- to eight-course meals in the evenings. At noon they can indulge in a three- or a four-course meal.

Öffnungszeiten:
Di - Sa
18.30 - 21.30 Uhr

Alle Kreditkarten akzeptiert

Opening hours:
Tue - Sat
6.30 pm - 9.30 pm

All credit cards accepted

Guide MICHELIN

18 GAULT&MILLAU

A LA CARTE 95

falstaff 96

SENNS.RESTAURANT IM GUSSWERK
Söllheimerstrasse 16, Objekt 6, 5020 Salzburg
Tel. +43 664 / 4540 232
info@SENNS.Restaurant, www.senns.restaurant

STEIN

Hotel, Restaurant & Rooftop Bar

Restaurant & Hotel Guide

„Salzburg meets Venice“ lautet die Philosophie hinter dem Hotel Stein. So finden sich zahlreiche Akzente der beiden Kunst- und Kulturstädte in den Räumlichkeiten, angefangen von Leuchten und Glaskunstwerken der venezianischen Glasmanufaktur Barovier & Toso über Bilder des in Salzburg ansässigen Kunstfotografen Luigi Caputo bis hin zu Stoffen von Rubelli. Kompromisslos wurde im Hotel Stein Besonderes geschaffen. Und ebenso kompromisslos wird Qualität gelebt. Fine Food und prickelnder Champagner werden im beeindruckenden Seven Senses serviert. Das Restaurant & Rooftop Bar spricht wortwörtlich alle Sinne an und vereint ein modernes Konzept mit gehobenen Ansprüchen. Für Momente, die in Erinnerung bleiben ...

"Salzburg meets Venice", that's the philosophy behind Hotel Stein, which was just reopened in 2018. Each of the two arts and culture cities has left traces all over the hotel, starting with lamps and works of art made by the Venetian glass manufactory Barovier & Toso, all the way to pictures by Salzburg-based fine art photographer Luigi Caputo to fabrics by Rubelli. Without compromise Hotel Stein was created to be special. And quality is embraced in an equally uncompromising fashion.
At Seven Senses, fine food and sparkling champagne are served on the new restaurant & rooftop Bar. Seven Senses is literally appealing to all senses and combines a modern concept with sophisticated demands. For unforgettable moments...

Öffnungszeiten:
01. Mai - 31. Aug:
täglich von 7 - 24 Uhr

01. Sep - 30. Apr:
Mo - Do 7 - 12 Uhr &
17 - 24 Uhr
Fr & Sa 7 - 24 Uhr
So 7 -17 Uhr

Frühstück 7 - 12 Uhr,
Brunch 11 - 17 Uhr,
warme Küche bis 22 Uhr

Opening hours:
01. May - 31. Aug:
daily 7 am - midnight

01. Sep - 30. Apr:
Mon - Thu 7 am - noon &
5 pm - midnight
Fri & Sat 7 am - midnight
So 7 am - 5 pm

Breakfast 7 am - noon,
brunch 11 am - 5 pm,
warm food served
until 10 pm

HOTEL STEIN
Giselakai 3 – 5, 5020 Salzburg
Tel. +43 662 / 8743 460
info@hotelstein.at, www.hotelstein.at

RESTAURANT SEVEN SENSES
Giselakai 3 – 5, 5020 Salzburg
Tel. +43 662 / 8772 77
info@7-senses.at, www.7-senses.at

TOWNHOUSE NORA

Restaurant & Hotel Guide

Boutique-Apartments by Heym Collections

Membership: Pretty Hotels

Fünf Gehminuten von der Linzergasse, im Andräviertel, entzückt eine Stadtvilla aus 1900 mit fünf sehr charmant eingerichteten Apartments. Den anspruchsvollen Gast erwartet gleich bei der Ankunft ein inspirierendes „Heym“: Jeder Raum lässt seine individuelle Seele und Ausstrahlung spüren, die sich aus ausgewählten antiken Stücken, hochwertiger Ausstattung und schönen Wandfarben ergibt. In den luxuriösen Boxspringbetten und Badezimmern lässt es sich herrlich vom Tag in der Stadt entspannen. Im größten Apartment gibt es sogar eine freistehende Badewanne. Geheimtipps über Salzburg gibt es vom 24/7-Concierge. Zubuchbar sind tolle Services wie ein Frühstückskorb oder Babysitter.

Only five minutes from Linzergasse and in the middle of Salzburg's Andräviertel quarter this delightful townhouse from 1900 offers five beautifully furbished apartments. Upon arrival the demanding guests immediately find an inspiring "Heym" or "home": each room has an individual soul and atmosphere that's characterised by selected antiques, high-quality furbishings, and beautifully coloured walls. The luxurious boxspring beds and bathrooms are perfect for a relaxed time after a day in the city. The largest apartment even has a freestanding tub. The 24/7 concierge has the best secret tips for Salzburg. And great services like a breakfast basket or babysitter can be booked, too.

TOWNHOUSE NORA
Schallmooser Hauptstrasse 17a, 5020 Salzburg
Tel. +43 664 / 1389 000
home@heymcollections.com, www.heymcollections.com

WIESERGUT

Designhotel mit legerem Luxus im Salzburger Land

Restaurant & Hotel Guide

Wenn sich die schmiedeeiserne Tür zum Wiesergut öffnet, der Blick auf puristische Architektur und hochwertige Materialien fällt, dann ist der Alltag schnell vergessen. Sepp und Martina Kröll, die Gastgeber des Designhotels im Glemmtal, haben mit dem Wiesergut einen Wohlfühlort für alle Sinne geschaffen. Zwischen den majestätischen Gipfeln der Kitzbüheler Alpen und der Hohen Tauern kann man wunderbar neue Energie schöpfen – sei es beim E-Biken, beim Wandern durch die unberührte Bergwelt, beim Sonnetanken auf der Wieseralm oder im hoteleigenen Wellnessbereich mit Infinitypool.
Für Gaumenfreuden sorgt Küchenchef Andrè Stahl, der mit Produkten aus der familiengeführten Landwirtschaft geschmackliche wie optische Kunstwerke zaubert.

As soon as the wrought-iron door of Wiesergut opens, your gaze settles on an environment of purist architecture and high-quality materials that quickly makes you forget everday life. Sepp and Martina Kröll, the hosts at the design hotel in Glemmtal valley, have made Wiesergut a space of wellbeing for all the senses. Tucked away between the majestic peaks of the Kitzbühel Alps and Hohe Tauern mountain range, this is the perfect place to recharge one's battery – during an e-bike tour, a hike through the mountains, while enjoying the sunshine on Wieseralm, or in the hotel's own spa area with infinity pool. Chef de cuisine André Stahl is in charge of satisfying the palate – with products from the family-owned farm that are turned into beautiful and tasty works of art.

Besondere Übernachtunsgsangebote finden Sie unter www.wiesergut.com/arrangements

For special package deals, see www.wiesergut.com/arrangements

Memberships:
Hideaway Hotels
Design Hotels

WIESERGUT GMBH & CO.KG FAMILIE KRÖLL
Wiesern 48, 5754 Hinterglemm
Tel. +43 6541 / 6308
info@wiesergut.com, www.wiesergut.com

IMPRESSUM/IMPRINT

2. Ausgabe La Loupe
Salzburg Stadt & Land
Sommerausgabe 2019
ISBN: 978-3-96443-959-8

Medieninhaber & Herausgeber:
La Loupe GmbH
Rennweg 32
6020 Innsbruck
Österreich

Tel. +43 664/5413 907
office@laloupe.com
www.laloupe.com

ATU 7099 2928
FN: 4525 71x

Geschäftsführung:
Benjamin Skardarasy

Redaktion:
Christina Knauseder-Csipek,
www.knauseders.at
Julia Skardarasy,
La Loupe GmbH
Benjamin Skardarasy,
La Loupe GmbH

Gestaltung & Layout:
Katrin Menga,
www.gestaltunghochzwei.de
Anna Horst,
www.annahorst.com
Julia Skardarasy,
La Loupe GmbH

Übersetzung:
Lisa Berger,
www.lisa-berger.at
Daniel Stevens

Lektorat:
Julia Stubenböck

Anzeigenverkauf:
Harald Genstorfer
hg@laloupe.com
+43 676 / 7223 581

Projektmanagement:
Julia Skardarasy,
La Loupe GmbH
Benjamin Skardarasy,
La Loupe GmbH

Druck:
Holzhausen Druck GmbH
Wienerfeldstraße 9
2120 Wolkersdorf,
Österreich

Fotonachweis:
*La Loupe, Copyrights der Advertorial-Bilder und Anzeigen-Bilder liegen bei den Kunden.

NOTIZEN / *NOTES*